NEW ENGLAND
TIKI

KEVIN QUIGLEY

THE
History
PRESS

Published by The History Press
Charleston, SC
www.historypress.com

First published 2023

Manufactured in the United States

ISBN 9781467153096

Library of Congress Control Number: 2022951594

It is not down in any map; true places never are.

—*Herman Melville,* Moby-Dick

For Gabriel Bascom and Xtine Benoit: Wusong Wednesdays forever.

CONTENTS

ACKNOWLEDGEMENTS

No book is written alone, and that goes triple for a nonfiction book. First off, thanks to my Wusong Wednesday crew: Xtine Benoit, Gabriel Bascom, John Shin, Joe Rinaldi, Andy Boimila, Matt Tetrault, Curtis Miller, Stephen Hagen, and, of course, Jason Doo. The New England Tiki Society, especially Joe and Ren Provo, Bob Gouveia, Frank Dukette, Captain Pat Lochelt and Joy Lochelt, and Mark "Trader Duck" Poutenis. All the folks who were generous enough to be interviewed, including Sven Kirsten, Otto Von Stroheim, and James and Bridget Kathary. Scott Schell, who was extraordinarily generous with his picture collection; Annene Kaye-Berry for her crucial help with Orchids of Hawaii information; and her husband, Jeff "Beachbum" Berry, for all his work on tiki and cocktail history.

Thanks to Jeff Covello for taking me on my first of many tiki crawls; Joe Yost, who introduced me to my first Trader Vic's; Matt and Kira Weier and our adventures with Tiki McBoatface; Jordan Duncan; Matt Stroud; Matt Parrish, who let me do a tiki takeover of our *Thirty20Eight* podcast and who I finally met at Three Dots and a Dash in Chicago; everyone who donated to my GoFundMe; everyone who ever gifted me a tiki mug; and all the tiki bartenders who have ever served me: you're doing Donn's work, and I couldn't thank you enough.

Thank you to Brother Cleve, without whom this book wouldn't have been possible. Rest in peace, my kind and wonderful friend.

And my husband, Shawn Hill: my constant partner through life, my rock, my love. Even if his idea of a proper cocktail involves more slush than rum.

INTRODUCTION

I was barely twenty-one the first time I had my first tiki drink. Well, that's stretching it a little. I was at a karaoke night with my friend Jim somewhere in suburban Massachusetts, and the place was serving Chinese food and "exotic cocktails." Jim and I split a pupu platter, in part because it came on a platter shaped like a volcano, with a divot on top for Sterno. I've long been a sucker for fried food dipped in sweet sauce, especially if it was served to me on fire. Jim also ordered a scorpion bowl, and though I was a teetotaler most of my young adult life, I consented. Something to do with the novelty of drinking from comically long straws. Did I like it? Man, *did* I. Syrupy-sweet with just the barest touch of alcohol. Exactly what a kid who had no experience with drinking might want. I also got a little tipsy, which was fairly unusual to me. I don't think I liked that part of it. For much of my adolescence and young adulthood, I was too tightly wound to ever really be on island time.

Flash forward to 2019. Over two decades had passed, and I found myself in California with my travel buddy Jeff. We'd met through a mutual love of Disney parks, and we were both enamored of the Enchanted Tiki Room—the in-park attraction where the birds sing words and the flowers croon—and the Trader Sam's bars in both domestic Disney resorts (the one in Walt Disney World is officially called Trader Sam's Grog Grotto, and it's a part of the Polynesian Village Resort, another Disney tiki place I was inordinately fond of). I still wasn't a big drinker, but I'd developed a taste for coconut rum and pineapple juice over the years. This, combined with my love of Disney's faux-Polynesian spaces, convinced Jeff that while we were in California, we needed to go on a tiki bar crawl. He knows the sort of themed entertainment that makes me giddy. Tiki, as it turns out, makes me giddy.

I was in San Francisco for work, but when the night came, we would start to hit bars. As I said, I started off my adulthood teetotaling, so the very concept of a bar crawl was novel and a little scary to me. I hadn't been in a bar regularly since my husband and I stopped going to the scene bars in Boston once domesticity swaddled us in its clinging, soft embrace. What I didn't know then was that San Francisco was one of the loci of both the original tiki explosion in post-Prohibition California and the tiki resurgence that started taking hold in the late 1990s. I was just going because it seemed like a neat experience, another aspect of that Midcentury Modern thing I was so all about. I didn't know it was going to be an inflection point.

In San Francisco, we visited Smuggler's Cove, a three-story tiki paradise with two bars and exceptional theming. Everything felt like it was under water. The walls and ceiling were festooned with nautical bric-a-brac. A small fountain lit from within burbled under a staircase on the lower level, glowing blue and adding to the ethereal feel of the murk of the place. The drink menu sprawled out before me, with names like Aku-Aku and Three Dots and a Dash and Doctor Funk. All of it was strange, the first new drink language I would have to learn since discovering that Starbucks was using fake Italian for beverage sizes, a concept that charmed me so much I learned to like coffee.

As it turned out, I liked tiki drinks. I liked the Sidewinder's Fang. I liked the Jet Pilot. And once we got our fill at Smuggler's Cove, we lit out for a jungle-themed bar called Last Rites that purported to be the ruins of a downed commercial airplane in a remote jungle island. The place smelled of burned cinnamon and adventure. The seats were 1950s airplane seats. Giant skulls glowed from the dark walls. It was feeling more and more like a new world was opening up to me, a world removed from the Disney fantasies I'd always loved—but not that removed. The Tiki Room, the entire concept of Adventureland, the Jungle Cruise—those were influenced by places like these in the 1930s and '40s and '50s, and here we were, full circle, with revival bars and restaurants at least in part influenced by Disney's concepts.

We headed to the Tonga Room, the legendary establishment in the basement of the Fairmont Hotel. A lagoon that dominates the room hosts musicians on a floating barge, and every once in a little while, thunder rumbles and lightning flashes and there's a rain shower inside. How did this happen at places outside Disney? What magic had gripped these bars that made them so astounding? My world travel so far had supported my Disney habit. Yes, Jeff and I went to Tokyo to see Tokyo…but we also spent a lot of time at Tokyo Disneyland. Ditto Paris, ditto Hong Kong. This was something entirely different. This was going to a regular, normal city and finding a lushly themed environment hidden away, ready to make your dreams of adventure come true. Were there any places like this back home in Boston?

From San Francisco, we moved to Palm Springs, booking a room in a Midcentury Modern motel called the Orbit In—yes, with one *n*—and the whole thing was atomic age poptimism at every turn. Seriously, from the amoeba clock on the wall to the Formica table to the rocket ship–shaped ice bucket in the living room, our whole room looked like a Charles Phoenix fever dream come to plastic life. Maybe that's another reason tiki draws me in. It doesn't look or feel like the futurism that excites me so much about the aesthetic of the 1950s, but the whole Polynesian thing existed at the same time, for the same people. Tiki and Midcentury Modern are connected, and not just because they share that curious architectural touchstone, the jutting A-frame. Already I was thinking about tiki history, and why it happened when it did, and why it seemed to be happening again.

Palm Springs, and the continuation of our tiki crawl. First, a trip to the Tonga Hut, which was nice, but I didn't know about the hidden room, and we drank out on the balcony instead of in the themed indoors, and there was karaoke happening. Then, The Reef at Caliente Tropics, a semi-seedy tiki-themed hotel with one of the more classic tiki bars on the West Coast. They were silently playing episodes of *Magnum, P.I.* on the TV and playing yacht rock overhead, and while it wasn't the tiki sounds of classic exotica or more modern surf rock or hulabilly, I was very into the smooth sounds of Christopher Cross and Michael McDonald. The bar was lit up gorgeously in blue, and the bartender, who had a way with a Nui Nui and a Rum Runner, was kind enough to tell us about Bootlegger Tiki, just up the road a piece.

Ah, the Bootlegger Tiki, dark inside, swathed in red as though we were in the glow of a volcano. Gorgeously low-brow black-velvet paintings of half-nude wahines hung on the walls, while Jeff and I hung at the bar, sipping drinks with complicated, thrilling garnishes, like tropical hideaways in a ceramic tiki mug. Was this my fifth drink of the night? Sixth? It didn't matter. Waiting for me at the end of the night was a Mid-Mod hotel room in the shadow of the San Jacinto Mountains, and I was perfectly happy to be squiffy in a place like that.

Los Angeles followed. We couldn't miss the Tiki-Ti, even though at the time I wasn't quite aware of the deep tiki history in which I was imbibing.

That would change. We ended our trip at Disneyland and the original Trader Sam's. Jeff by then was sick of rum. I was just getting started. My brain was on fire. I wanted to know everything about tiki, about these fake Polynesian places, all the whys and wherefores. Later that year, I went on my long-delayed honeymoon, and I did it in Hawai'i, where my husband and I could actually look out on the waters of the South Pacific, and I could see some of the "real" influences behind these artificial spots back on the mainland.

Back home in Boston, I started seriously to think about my home and what sort of tiki was to be found there. After all, the places I'd been in California were darn near tropical already. Didn't a place like New England *need* exotic escapes more than those West Coasters did? I started to read books on the subject (the first being *California Tiki*, by Jason Henderson and Adam Foshko, part of this very series). Then the pandemic hit, and I was stuck inside for days at a time. There were days in which sometimes all I had to do was read books about tiki history: Sven Kirsten's *The Book of Tiki*, Beachbum Berry's *Sippin' Safari*, all the History Press tiki books, more and more. I'd had no idea there was so much material on tiki history, tiki architecture, and tiki mixology just out there, waiting to be studied by an eager novice. But it occurred to me that virtually none of the books I read, none of the resources I consulted, talked about tiki in New England. Once in a while, they would mention Kowloon, the giant pan-Asian restaurant in Saugus, Massachusetts, out on Route 1, but it usually only got a passing glance. Was there really no tiki history here?

There was. And there had been. And there was about to be. In New England, tiki was all over, but it didn't assert itself. We Yankees like to keep things close to the vest, and we like to do things our own way, and that includes our faux-tropical hideaways.

If New England tiki was going to be found, it would have to be done by a curious, patient, and persistent tiki aficionado.

That's where I come in.

FROM PILGRIMS TO PROHIBITION

A SHORT HISTORY OF NEW ENGLAND, BOATS, AND RUM

T he *Mayflower* landed on Plymouth Rock in 1620, carrying scores of British refugees, Pilgrims, in search of the New World. They were over five thousand miles away from Hawai'i, six thousand miles from Tahiti, and nine thousand miles from New Zealand. The first nonnative settlers in this place that would eventually become America, these Pilgrims were about as far away from the South Pacific as someone could get. Tiki fever wouldn't hit these shores for a few more centuries. In centuries to come, we would celebrate another European, Christopher Columbus, as the discoverer of America—although he really landed in the Caribbean, ironically a region that would become very important in the world of tiki. But all that comes later.

America, our young country, was born by the sea, and New England— Massachusetts (including the portion that would later secede and become Maine), Vermont, Connecticut, New Hampshire, and Rhode Island—grew from maritime roots. Fishing and coastal timber were immediate industries, and the British, facing domestic timber depletion, harvested liberally from Maine to make impressive ships' masts for their growing navy. Islands off the coast of Maine became thriving settlements, with their shores teeming with fish for food and trade. Island time in early Maine was less palm trees and tropical surf and more granite mining and massive deforestation. They couldn't even relax with a tasty Mai Tai, which wouldn't be invented for over a century.

Soon enough, the lower New England colonies—Massachusetts, Connecticut, Rhode Island—realized how intense the fervor was for their resources and began building their own ships. The demand for shipbuilding was so great that British citizens immigrated to America to take part in the shipbuilding boom. From the start, New England was renowned for its ties to the sea, and those ties grew stronger even as the Revolutionary War and the War of 1812 took a toll on both production and demand.

Then there's whaling, a vastly important industry in New England's growth and early prosperity. Whale oil—especially the spermaceti, a waxy substance found in the heads of sperm whales—was used in gas lamps, whale bones for clothing and furniture, whale teeth for the curious craft of scrimshaw, and of course, ambergris, a bile found in whale intestine, was highly coveted for use in perfumes. Ambergris was so sought after that in the 1880s, two ounces (equal to the ounces of Virgin Island rum in a Nui Nui!) went for $10,000, literally worth its weight in gold.

Massachusetts's Buzzards Bay was the first center of the whaling economy in the new United States, but other ports in Massachusetts—Martha's Vineyard, Barnstable, Nantucket, not to mention ports in Connecticut and Rhode Island—became hubs of the industry. It is from Nantucket that the whaleship *Essex* sailed and was later sunk by a whale. Its fictional counterpart, the *Pequod*, also sails from Nantucket on the hunt for the great white whale Moby-Dick. Whether due to its maritime history or the ongoing reverence for and study of *Moby-Dick*, whales became and have remained a figure in tiki culture. As recently as 2021, Tikiland Trading created a fine and immense whale mug, as beautiful a piece of art as tiki mugs come; in 2022, Disney achieved a similar feat with its Monstro mug. I have both on my mug shelves, right next to a copy of *Moby-Dick*. Mine is a New England tiki collection.

One can't discuss the early history of New England without discussing rum, eventually one of the cornerstones of American tiki. Rum was one of the colonies' chief initial industries, with over 150 distilleries making good use of the millions of gallons of imported Caribbean molasses. Well, by "imported," I mean "smuggled." Domestic rum production was massively important to New England's economy, and the British knew it. As New Englanders turned to the French for their molasses needs, as it was far cheaper than the British stuff, the British levied a hefty tax on any imported molasses, sugar, and rum. The Molasses Act of 1733 would either force the colonies to buy British molasses, British sugar, British rum, or it would decimate the New England rum industry. A win-win for the British! Except not really.

At first, New Englanders protested against the unseemly act. Then they realized that pirates sailed these waters, too, and if doing things the legal way was going to destroy them, they might as well work with master smugglers. Pirates smuggled at least half the molasses that came into New England as these new Americans essentially ignored British law. The more insidious Sugar Act of 1764 was a lot more successful, but New Englanders kept working with pirates for their molasses. While beer and baked beans and curing meat were important early uses for molasses, the production of rum was paramount. New England loved its favorite libation: by the mid-1700s, Massachusetts supported sixty-three distilleries, Rhode Island thirty, and together they produced about 1,200,000 gallons of rum annually.

Schoolchildren are often taught the gruesome history of all that rum, the "triangular trade" being easy to understand and hard to forget. Slaves from West Africa would be abducted to the West Indies (where rum was probably invented and given the evocative name "kill-devil"), where they would toil on sugar plantations in order to make molasses to send to New England. The molasses came to New England to make kill-devil, which was then exported to Africa to trade for more slaves. Barbaric and hellish…and probably not true.

America was definitely involved in the slave trade, and Rhode Island did attempt to take part in this molasses-to-rum-to-slaves proposition. Nicholas Brown Sr., a Providence merchant who was attempting to raise funds for an iron foundry, sent out three slaver ships to Africa to trade for rum. One, the *Sally*, was beset by a slave uprising, sickness, starvation, and drowning. Another ship was lost at sea, and the third made only a meager profit. Human suffering and slavery on any scale are abhorrent, and at least 100,000 people were brought to New England, abducted from their homeland, and forced into labor in America. But the idea that the triangular trade was one of the backbones of New England's early prosperity is largely a myth. And an exploitable myth, at that, as we'll soon see.

Rum and ships, ships and rum. On and on, with New England building on its own definition of maritime, its own history of island life, its own economies on the shore of a vast ocean. The Gilded Age of the mid- to late 1800s swept America, ushering in industrialization and economic growth in the Northeast and beyond. Also growing? The parallel and sometimes entwined temperance and abolitionist movements. As the Civil War loomed, southerners who opposed abolitionism spoke about the triangular trade as an egregious hypocrisy on the part of New Englanders, suggesting that because their fortunes had already been made on the backs of enslaved Africans, abolition was mainly a selfish economic tactic. That the country had accepted the trade as fact lay largely on three works by historians George H. Moore, George C. Mason, and William B. Weeden, the two former of which vaguely suggested the idea without concluding evidence, then extrapolated by the latter in a lecture that invented facts out of whole cloth. Historian George McCusker argues that the idea gained traction due to a "morbid and somewhat flagellant fascination on the part of late nineteenth century New Englanders with the sins of their forefathers." To be fair, New Englanders never really lost this gift.

In 1919, as the first World War was nearing its end, something happened in Boston's North End that seemed a harbinger for the temperance movement's final hold on America's drinking. A massive molasses tank at the Purity Distilling Company suddenly burst, sending over two million gallons of molasses surging out and into the city. Poorly designed rivets, a hastily constructed tank, and the city's low temperatures (which had the effect of making the tank's steel brittle) all combined with general negligence to rupture the tank and send a tsunami of the sickly sweet liquid into the streets. Not all the molasses was used for rum and other alcohol; much of it was turned into ethanol to help build munitions for the Great War. But by 1919, Prohibition had already been ratified and was going into effect in 1920. New England had a long history with molasses and rum, and this flood—which killed 21 people, injured 150 more, and actually knocked buildings off their foundations and pushed a truck into Boston Harbor—must have seemed like vindication.

Not that Prohibition stopped New England's obsession with rum. As the Eighteenth Amendment went into effect, New Englanders once again took to the sea. Rum Row—a series of ships loaded with illegal hooch, anchored off the coast just beyond the maritime limit—turned Massachusetts port towns into hubs for smuggling. It was a return to the historical practice begun when the British levied their Molasses Act; once again, pirates earned a little extra money supplying rum to the colonists. Salisbury and Newburyport (known as the Clipper City) in particular became hot spots, sending small speedboats out to meet with larger craft on technically international waters—three miles offshore, eventually extended to twelve—laden with rum and other spirits from Canada and the Caribbean.

Rumrunning wasn't the only illegal industry that took hold during Prohibition: bootlegging, racketeering, and widespread corruption erupted as direct results of the ban on alcohol. Massachusetts could have learned something from the state of Maine, which had attempted statewide prohibition in 1851, a massive failure that gave rise to illegal saloons and eventually ended in a hail of gunfire known as the Portland Rum Riot. (This was also wrapped up in Portland mayor Neal Dow's hatred of the Irish and their so-called notorious groggeries, which would be an excellent name for an exotica band.) When the nation as a whole officially went dry, New England, as it had done with the Molasses Act, kind of ignored the law. In fact, Connecticut and Rhode Island refused to ratify the amendment. It's no surprise, really, that by 1921, Connecticut hosted 1,500 speakeasies, with 400 in New Haven alone.

Given New England's proximity to Canada, where liquor was still legal, speakeasies near the border sprang up, like Queen Lill's Bucket of Blood in Vermont; Queen Lill also did a brisk business in prostitutes, if you wanted to make a whole night of it. Hooch traveled through the unguarded forest roads from our neighbors to the north and into New Hampshire, Vermont, and Maine, which by now had some practice with wet workarounds. Some speakeasies—also known as line houses—not only bumped up against the Canadian border but actually straddled it. The Canaan Line House's front door opened onto Richford, Vermont, and its back door opened on Quebec.

While not the richly themed environments that tiki bars and restaurants would eventually bring to the region, these speakeasies proved that New Englanders had a taste and desire for hidden spaces where one could find drinks available nowhere else. In 1929, the stock market crashed, plunging America into the Great Depression. Joblessness reached epidemic proportions, and people who'd lost their homes erected shantytowns called Hoovervilles all over the Northeast and beyond. Our newly dry country offered little in the way of escape from the daily struggle of regular people trying to navigate their way through the hard times. It might be a stretch to say that there's a direct line between New England's line houses and speakeasies and the tiki culture that would eventually reach our Atlantic shores, but there is an echo from one era to another. Secret places, removed from reality, offered an escape to somewhere entirely different, if only for a little while.

As Prohibition sputtered out its last dry breaths in 1933, it seemed that all that rumrunning had left a surplus of the stuff behind. Though no one in New England knew it yet, an enterprising world traveler and raconteur known as Donn Beach had a plan for all that rum. On the other side of the country, where dreams were made on the silver screen, the first era of tiki in America was about to erupt in a rhapsody of rum—and it wouldn't be long before New England got its first taste.

Chapter 1

A ZOMBIE AT THE FAIR

Our story starts, as do most stories of tiki in America, with a man known as Donn Beach. Born Ernest Raymond Beaumont Gantt in 1907, Beach soon caught the adventurer's wanderlust, traveling from his home in the cultural melting pot of New Orleans to such far-flung locales as the Caribbean, the South Pacific, Cuba, Singapore, and more. Was he involved in rumrunning? Who can say? But as Prohibition ended and the public appetite for liquor was at a fever pitch, Donn Beach had enough rum on hand to open a bar—and, in doing so, created the template for American tiki.

In 1933, Donn purchased a vacated tailor's shop in Hollywood and turned it into a tiny, thirteen-by-thirty-foot bar, with twenty-four seats and a few tables. Throughout his years in Polynesia and beyond, Donn had accumulated scores of artifacts and ephemera, and he used everything he had as décor for his new watering hole. A sign reading "Don's Beachcomber" hung on the outside, inviting guests in for an experience like no other.

The Hollywood crowd ate it up—and drank it up. A desire for all things tropical had been growing in the national zeitgeist. A craze for Hawaiian music had erupted in the early twentieth century as the "exotic" sounds of the steel guitar and the ukulele made their way onto mainland records, plays, and vaudeville acts. In 1915, the Panama-Pacific International Exhibition featured a Hawai'i pavilion promoting music and tourism, and it captured the American imagination.

Exotic-styled nightclubs emerged; the concept of a tropical bar in and of itself was not really Donn Beach's innovation. In fact, two different nightclubs called Cocoanut Grove had opened on opposite coasts, both exemplars of the Roaring Twenties ethos. The Los Angeles–based location, opened in 1921, was a mishmash of "exotic" cultures, with Chinese and Arabian lanterns, towering palm trees, and mechanical monkeys overlaying a traditional high-end nightclub experience.

Boston's version opened in 1927 on Piedmont Street in the Bay Village by entertainer Mickey Alpert and musician Jacques Renard. Opened as it was during Prohibition, the Grove operated as a supper club; entertainer-owners Alpert and Renard were both convinced that the live music and other amusements would draw visitors even without the prospect of alcohol. Their lofty optimism didn't take into account their inexperience in running a nightclub, nor did it account for the fact that their financier, Jacob Berman (aka Jack Bennett), was a swindler responsible for defrauding Los Angeles oil investors to the tune of $100 million. Upon learning of this, Alpert and Renard decided to finance the Grove themselves, another unexpected expense that edged them closer to bankruptcy. With its large dining area, dance floor with bandstand, and several bar areas, the day-to-day operations grew more expensive than its co-owners could manage on their own. Bowing to financial pressure, they sold the nightclub to notorious local gangster Charles "King" Solomon in 1931 for $10,000.

King Solomon, one of New England's first major crime figures, deviated from Alpert and Renard's temperance pledge almost immediately. With a background in narcotics smuggling and bootlegging, Solomon turned the Cocoanut Grove into a speakeasy whose habitués were other gangsters. The nightclub gained a seedy reputation, one that Solomon tried to combat with an air of respectability. "It means everything to me," he said of the club. "I've had enough of the hard and the rotten and miserable. I was always a bum to nice people. Now, when I put on those evening clothes and step through the door of the Cocoanut Grove, I'm a gentleman. I'm not a heel, you understand, I'm their host." A host, incidentally, who controlled all New England's illegal gambling and who had previously been suspected of running a massive intercontinental rumrunning ring with three fellow gangsters.

The grittiness of the Grove was a reputation that might have further plagued the club had King Solomon not visited the Cotton Club in late January 1933 (incidentally, the same year Donn Beach opened his tiny bar in Los Angeles on the other coast). Owned by restaurateur and nightclub impresario Tommy Maren, the Cotton Club was a local bar catering to

Angelo Lippi, maître d' of Cocoanut Grove. *National Fire Protection Association.*

Boston's Black community and the late-night scene. On that fateful night, King Solomon left his female companions at a table to go use the restroom and was followed by a group of men at a nearby table. An argument ensued, and gunshots shattered the ambience of the club. When Solomon lurched out of the restroom, witnesses saw he had been shot in the chest, the abdomen, and the neck. He died a short time later in the hospital, living long enough to explain that he'd been gunned down by "those dirty rats."

Boston's Cocoanut Grove then fell into the hands of Barney Welansky, Solomon's lawyer, who had grand plans for the location. Perhaps using the Los Angeles namesake as inspiration, Welansky similarly festooned *his* Cocoanut Grove with towering fake palm trees and light fixtures made to look like coconuts. Rattan and bamboo covered the walls, and draperies and canopies hung from walls and ceilings. In the summer months, the ceiling could be rolled back, and patrons could dance under the stars. Former co-owner Mickey Alpert became the club's emcee, and eventually, the Grove began to attract mainstream musical acts, movie stars, and the elite of Boston society. But despite the club's new South Seas appearance and outward theater of respectability, the Cocoanut Grove was still a gangster hangout. It was also a powder keg. Welansky, who had ties not only with the Mafia but also then-mayor Maurice J. Tobin, routinely flouted building codes. His exotic-seeming palm trees were highly flammable. Ditto the gorgeous looking but cheap ceiling canopies. And he nailed some exit doors shut so customers couldn't sneak out without paying for drinks. *Powder keg.*

Still, both these nightclubs with their exotic ambiance and décor certainly *looked* beautiful, the epitome of Jazz Age glitz and glamor—which was exactly the opposite of what Donn Beach was aiming for in his bar. Despite the feints toward the exotic, both versions of the Cocoanut Grove were ostensibly high-class establishments in which fancy dress was the mode of the day and spacious dance floors were filled with folks dancing to standards.

On the other hand, Don's Beachcomber was dark and intimate, living and breathing its exotic atmosphere rather than wearing it like a costume. Ironic, as Don's Beachcomber was *all* costume. Opening as it had during the Great Depression, Donn's bar was about as close to the South Pacific as anyone was going to get. It wasn't as if the folks scrambling for jobs could afford a ticket to Tahiti. They let Tahiti—and Bora Bora, and Hawai'i, and more—come to them, in the form of this dark and seemingly authentic experience just off Hollywood Boulevard. What Beach was inventing was later defined as both "pre-tiki" and "Polynesian pop" by tiki historian Sven Kirsten. "Pre-tiki" because the thing for which tiki bars are named—carved wooden idols with roots in actual Polynesia—had yet to emerge as the defining characteristic of the South Seas bar, and "Polynesian pop," which is a sort of catch-all phrase for the American (especially mainland) interpretation of this type of exotic ambiance. Beach's tropical South Seas experience was only the beginning.

The touch of the exotic may have brought many of Donn's patrons in, but what kept them coming back were the drinks, what he termed his "Rhum Rhapsodies" (the spelling here is largely whimsical; in the strictest sense, *rum* is a catch-all term for any variety of the spirit, most of which are derived from molasses; *rhum*, short for *rhum agricole*, a French term meaning *agricultural rum*, is distilled from fermented, fresh-pressed juice from sugar cane—no molasses included. Donn Beach offered all types of rums and rhums in his establishment; he just thought the "h" looked cool.) The general public, who wouldn't know Maui from the Marquesas, had no idea that this seemingly realistic South Pacific experience was serving drinks far more tied to the Caribbean. In fact, the Caribbean cocktail adage and rhyme "one of sour, two of sweet, three of strong, four of weak" was the guiding principle on which Donn crafted his libations. (*Sour* was generally citrus, *sweet* was something like sugar syrup or falernum, *strong* was rum, *weak* was a balancing liquid like water.) They came with adventurous names like Vicious Virgin and Sidewinder's Fang and with ingredients designed to confound anyone who would attempt to steal his recipes. Privately, he had his bartenders concoct sweeteners and spices but clung tightly to the secret of what was in them. Thus, while a patron (or a recipe thief) might determine that a Nui Nui included amber rum (the strong) and several types of citruses (the sour), they would have no idea what to make of "Don's Spices #2." Ditto "Don's

Mix," "Don's Gardenia Mix," "Dashes #8," and so on. When the bar grew too popular to remain in the abandoned tailor's shop, Donn moved across the street and engineered even more mystery by having his four Filipino bartenders create his Rhapsodies in the back, away from the crowd. The sole bartender up front would pour the more traditional beverages—your martinis, your highballs—while your Beachcomber's Gold would appear from behind the shroud of mystery, complete with an ice shell like a frozen wave rising out of your glass and over your drink.

This sort of theatricality, lauded in Hollywood, extended beyond the drinks. As each night wore on, Donn would run outside and turn a hose on, splattering the tin roof; inside, guests who had been about to leave would hear the simulated rainstorm and decide to stay for another cocktail or two. It was marketing and showmanship rolled into one and a blending of so-called exotic that was part South Seas, part Caribbean, and part Hollywood invention. Donn even trucked in Haitian folklore when he introduced a drink called the Zombie, a beverage featuring three different types of rum, plus a little bit of Pernod, an anise-flavored absinthe substitute featuring wormwood, an extremely potent botanical. On his colorful menus, Donn would warn that he would serve only two Zombies per customer. What might happen if you imbibed more? Would you become a zombie? (The answer is yes.)

Advertising his Zombie as something halfway between a warning and a challenge, Donn attracted many would-be imitators, all of whom wanted to crack his secrets and serve their own versions. The man who would bring the Zombie to the East Coast was more enterprising than most and a lot more ambitious.

Monte Proser started off life as an "elegant hobo" before becoming a publicist to such Hollywood stars as Mary Pickford—the "It" girl—Harold Lloyd, and the Marx Brothers. But Proser had other ambitions, and when he saw the success Donn Beach was having with his establishment, he smelled opportunity. The 1939 New York World's Fair offered a perfect setting for his idea. Futurism was the theme of the day, with fair planners hoping that an escape into the world of tomorrow would raise people's spirits and hopes during the last gasps of the Great Depression. With its immense Streamline Moderne buildings of glass and chromium, the huge white globe of the Perisphere (which featured a model city of the future within), and the seven-hundred-foot Trylon obelisk towering over the fair and the city, it might seem that something like Donn Beach's tropical getaway concept would feel out of place.

Monte Proser's Zombie at the New York World's Fair 1940 postcard. *Scott Schell.*

On the contrary, because escapism was the watchword of the moment, guests at the fair were in the mood for a little exotic adventure mixed with their dreams of the future. With this in mind, Monte Proser decided to bring his "borrowed" idea of the South Seas bar to the World's Fair midway. An ad for the new establishment featured a "native" dancing in a mask and outfit of unknown origin, along with the cone-and-ball icon of the Trylon and the Perisphere; it read: "THE ZOMBIE GOES TO THE FAIR/TOMORROW/The most exciting idea of the Broadway Night Club season goes to the Fair…featuring its Drinks…its Gay Spirit…and the Tropical Atmosphere that has swept not only this town but the whole country./IT'S A MUST ON YOUR FAIR FUN LIST!"

The ad and the atmosphere worked; it really was a must on everyone's fair fun list. Monte Proser's Zombie Café was as immediate a hit on the East Coast as Donn Beach's bar had been on the West. Part of that had to with Proser deciding, in the most generous terms, not to mess with perfection. In the least generous terms, he basically stole the Don the Beachcomber concept wholesale, and as we'll see, he kept doubling down. With bamboo lettering down the side and an illustration flanked by palm trees depicting a "native jungle" scene, Proser's South Seas establishment proclaimed of the Zombie, "NO MORE THAN 2 PER CUSTOMER PLEASE," just as Donn Beach had on his menu. Flattery by way of blatant imitation, and Proser would not be content to confine his success to a robust but temporary fair. The entire East Coast awaited.

(Interestingly, another establishment at the fair, Ruby Foo's Sun Dial, provided New Yorkers with a different taste of the exotic with Foo's then-novel Chinese dishes, including chop suey and chow mein. Foo *also* had a version of the Zombie on her cocktail menu, portending a union in Rhode Island just a little farther on up the road.)

With his Zombie Café a proven hit, Proser decided to branch out. Not content to simply purloin Donn Beach's most famous drink, he took the actual name of Beach's bar—The Beachcomber—and opened a location in New York City, above the Winter Garden Theater. From there, he innovated

Zombie Café at the New York World's Fair. *Scott Schell.*

in one way that Donn himself had yet to capitalize on: Proser franchised. Monte Proser's Beachcomber bars began popping up everywhere. The rustic shack exterior (with a neon sign!) for New York translated into a World's Fair–type Streamline Moderne building in Miami Beach and a location in Baltimore, Maryland.

And this is when Polynesian pop finally landed in New England. Massachusetts, already primed for a taste of the tropics with its Cocoanut Grove (and Boston's habit of naming its nightclubs after those in Los Angeles), welcomed its first real taste of proto-tiki when Monte Proser's Beachcomber opened at 150 Boylston Street. Just six miles away from Cocoanut Grove and run under the "personal direction of Tommy Maren" (the owner of the Cotton Club, where King Solomon had so recently been gunned down), the Beachcomber offered similar experiences as its New York and Miami Beach locations, copying the Don the Beachcomber format all the way down to its reliance on Filipino bartenders. A *Boston Globe* ad—surrounded by a black border with the words "ZOMBIE * ZOMBIE * ZOMBIE" repeating in white type throughout—welcomed Legionnaires back to the city with the words "Okole maluna pali-pono which means in Island Language 'For Your Enjoyment.'" (It doesn't. *Okole maluna* means "Bottoms up!" *Pali* means "hill" and *pono* is a sort of farewell.)

A squib next to the Legionnaires' ad thrilled at the coming of Proser's Beachcomber: "THE BEACHCOMBER, Boylston Street, is one of the most startling replicas of a thatched roof hut on a Hawaiian beach and

Monte Proser's Beachcomber ad. *Scott Schell*

presents a floor show, dancing, and entertainment by native Hawaiians and food prepared by native chefs." The "native chefs" were almost certainly not Hawaiian; Proser and Maren seemed to predict the tiki tradition of serving Americanized Cantonese food with the Beachcomber's multiple chow mein and egg foo young options. There were also plenty of American dishes, including spring lamb chop, fresh lobster salad, and the distinctly Massachusetts offering of broiled fresh Boston scrod.

As for the entertainment, much of it was more in line with what the Cocoanut Grove offered. The "clown prince of comedy," Artie Dann, was a performer and an emcee; Latin performer Alberto Socarrás brought his "magic flute" and orchestra and offered rhumba lessons; and Lu-Cellia, the club's onetime featured artist, was a half-Castilian, half-Indian dancer who performed "in America's most savage dance spectacle." (Ad copy screamed: "Barbaric! Exotic! Authentic! Dynamic!") While a 1941 New Year's Eve ad ("Boston's gayest!") promised a "completely new tropical revue," I have been able to find no evidence that native Hawaiians actually performed there, which was somewhat odd, given the still-recent Hawaiian music craze. But the boast portended the direction that many Polynesian pop and tiki restaurants would hew toward in the future. As Sven Kirsten would later put it in *The Book of Tiki*, the aesthetic aims for "authentically inauthentic"; real luaus in fake Polynesia would fit that adage to a T.

Other ads proclaimed the Beachcomber the "Home of the Zombie," which was accurate, if you disregard which coast's Beachcomber Proser was talking about. Proser couldn't quite get away from naming at least part of his restaurants after the drink; in addition to the Tropical Garden, the Boston Beachcomber housed a Zombie Room and Terrace. The *Globe* ads touted the club's amenities with flowery South Seas prose, such as the valet service: "In the islands we can't be bothered worrying, we just try to eat and live as comfortably as possible….Parking your car has always been a worry. Simply drive up—give your car to our doorman—it will be parked in the Eliot Garage…you pay 25¢…we pay the rest…gladly."

The Zombie wasn't the only thing Proser lifted from Donn Beach's original concept. Other drinks were either inspired by or simply ripped off from Beach's menu, like the Vicious Virgin, the Pi Yi (served in a baby pineapple!), and the Planter's Punch. Touted as just some of the "SIXTY drinks from the Hot Countries," these would be sure to warm on cold New England nights when, for a little while, you could pretend the tropics were close.

The menus and ads played up the Beachcomber theme as readily as Donn had done; one of Proser's standard illustrations was that of a shirtless white man in ragged pants on a solitary desert island, leaning against a lone palm tree with a satisfied smile on his face. The Boston menus often featured bare-chested, full-grown women, as well as miniature women who were just as topless and just as buxom, fanning this man with palm fronds, offering him food and beverage, and simply admiring him. Exoticism mixed with male chauvinism was, unfortunately, an early component of tropical and Polynesian pop imagery. Also prominent? Overt racism and Orientalism. Some menus depict a Black doorman in a turban and a cape, either in a "sambo" style or in exaggerated blackface. One of the restaurant's main mascots was an invented character named "Chin," represented by an extreme caricature of a Chinese man in a red Mandarin cap, who served as the "No. 1 boy at The Beachcomber." Other attributes associated with Chin: he is the "possessor of the secret food recipes of the Ancient Islanders" (which islands?), he was "born the seventh son of a witch," and was "your most humble servant at all times." Elsewhere, the menu's wording spoke in broken English for further "authenticity."

Doubling down on these concepts was Ruby Foo, who owned the Providence, Rhode Island location of Proser's borrowed franchise. Foo was a fascinating figure in early twentieth-century New England: born close to the turn of the century—likely in San Francisco—Foo barely escaped poor debtor court to open a restaurant in Boston's Chinatown, probably around 1929. Called The Den, it offered only Cantonese fare, unlike many other Chinatown restaurants, which also offered traditional American food to entice all palates. But Foo's cuisine, exotic as it may have felt to early twentieth-century Bostonians, caught on—not just with the local Chinese population but with Caucasians, as well.

As the first woman in Chinatown to become a restaurateur, Foo's stable grew. Franchisees in New York City approached her first, and by 1936, a Den had opened on Broadway. Soon, she had a location in London, England, and of course she found a place at the New York World's Fair, where her Sun Dial restaurant served punches, cocktails, and that infamous libation, the Zombie. When Foo wanted to open a new location closer to home, she looked no farther than Monte Proser.

Proser's Beachcomber restaurants had been doing well, and sometime in the early 1940s, he expanded to Rhode Island. Providence's Crown Hotel was in the market for themed restaurant experiences, having already added the Deep Sea Cocktail Lounge, featuring murals of mermaids and a classic diving suit propped in one corner. The Beachcomber, sold to Ruby Foo in 1941, featured a "fantasia of Polynesian-patterned wall coverings, framed by bamboo." It was the first Polynesian pop restaurant to open inside a hotel anywhere in America, presaging the likes of Trader Vic's, Steven Crane's Kon-Tiki Ports, and any number of independent restaurants and cocktail lounges that would pair with hotels and motels as the tiki craze erupted in the next couple of decades. With three floor shows a night (at 8:00 p.m., 10:00 p.m., and midnight, often featuring the musical stylings of singer Don Marco and showgirl sextet the Beachcharmers), the restaurant more than justified its cover charge of one dollar, although the steep price of entry kept many servicemen in uniform out, despite their teeming presence at other local clubs.

Ruby Foo's Den restaurants were heavily themed, evoking China in their painted murals of mountains and seas and boasting ornate structural pagodas that, through the power of forced perspective, seemed to tower over diners. The artwork for the Boston menu continued the Chinese theming, featuring an image of an elegant Asian man with a Fu Manchu mustache, wearing a four-corner Fangjin hat and holding a red paper fan, obscuring part of his face.

The Crown Hotel location initially kept the basics of the Proser Beachcomber logo, including subservient island women kneeling by the Beachcomber and Chin on a separate island touting the "Brilliant Entertainment * Unusual Food * Choice Liquors," as an island woman in a flowing skirt and high heels dances nearby. Slowly, Foo improved on the basics, articulating the titular beachcomber more (he has hair now!) and adding more details such as a faraway island, a red setting sun, and people in an outrigger canoe paddling out to sea. The menu art eventually changed from the standard Beachcomber concept to fit in line with Foo's Chinese perspective, changing the beachcomber into a smiling Chinese man— something of a caricature in hanfu robes and a Mandarin cap—being served libations by a mermaid, while a monkey in a palm tree prepares to throw a coconut, disrupting the scene.

At points north, there was one final vestige of Monte Proser's New England tropical takeover. The 150-room Graymore Hotel had opened as the Brunswick, and changed its name as the building was expanded in 1923. The concept of exotically themed restaurants was not new to the neighborhood; the Morocco Lounge with its attendant columns and murals had opened in the 1930s at the nearby Wadsworth Hotel. The Beachcomber Room came to the Graymore in 1940, and it was a good fit, given the hotel's nautical iconography: an illustration of a Maine fisherman shining a lantern before him against the backdrop of a stylized sea under a puffy pillow of

Beachcomber Room, Hotel Graymore. *Scott Schell.*

clouds. "The Graymore Hotel," the souvenir matchbooks cried, "for Down-East Hospitality in Portland, Maine."

Maine's version of Monte Proser's Beachcomber was festooned with deep booths, tropical wall murals, and ersatz palm trees—standard décor for these early proto-tiki restaurants and lounges. Promising a place to "Dine and Dance," Portland's Beachcomber seemed eager to let you know that it was "Affiliated with Times Square Hotel, New York City," offering a touch of big-city class—or just making sure it stood out among the other hotel lounges on Preble Street in Portland. One of Hotel Graymore's flyers (or perhaps it was a placemat) for the Room presented the standard icon of the shirtless beachcomber leaning against a towering palm tree but with a decidedly *non*-standard lounging topless woman in a flimsy skirt, looking with some dismay at a photograph held in her outstretched hand. This raven-haired beauty is supported by a broken English phrase, clinging to the curves of her body: "So sorry…but camera do not lie!" One imagines that the dining and dancing might get so out of hand that photographers would be standing by to catch your every faux pas. A jolly night out in paradise, preserved forever!

Unfortunately, if there had been photographers on hand at the Beachcomber Room, the pictures haven't much surfaced. There are shockingly few surviving photos of these early rooms and lounges and only marginally more paper archives like mailers, matchbooks, and postcards. One contemporary of Monte Proser's chain, proprietor Artie McKenzie's Tropical Room in Providence, Rhode Island's Hotel Mohican, might as well never have existed. Other than a few newspaper mentions and a surviving matchbook, the Tropical Room—once touted as "R.I.'s Night Spot!"—has completely disappeared. Now, in a time when nearly every moment of every day is captured on digital photography, it is almost inconceivable to imagine that a whole swath of time can just be lost to the annals of history.

But photographs were not all that was lost: in 1941, the *Honolulu Star-Bulletin* reported that Donn Beach owned not only the Beachcomber name but also the name of Proser's first famous establishment and its attendant drink, the Zombie. "That potent threat to the sobriety of café society," the *Star-Bulletin* chuckled, "the Zombie legally ruled out of bounds in New York today." From New York, the cease-and-desist decree slipped into New England, targeting Boston and Rhode Island and eventually points south.

For his part, Proser was already moving on to bigger and more famous nightclubs. In late 1940, he, partnering with New York crime boss Frank Costello, opened the Copacabana near Fifth Avenue in New York City to rousing success. In Boston, the Beachcomber name stuck around for a while, even after officially dropping Proser's possessive above the name. In mid-1942, Tommy Maren grew the location, moving the kitchen to a lower floor and expanding the club to accommodate one hundred more patrons.

Everything, sadly, was about to change. On November 28, 1942, Boston's Cocoanut Grove was packed to the rafters. Following the death of Prohibition, the Grove had become one of Boston's most exciting hot spots. Football fans grieving that night's loss of Boston College to Holy Cross College at Fenway Park (55–12, a real rout) retreated to the Grove to drink their sorrows away. Hollywood cowboy and country music singer Buck Jones, traveling the country to raise money for war bonds, was in attendance. Though he was feeling poorly, his movie agents talked him, reluctantly, into making an appearance. The club's owner, Barney Welansky, had suffered a heart attack a little over a week before and was then recovering at Mass General Hospital nearby.

The fire began simply with a request to fix a lightbulb. In the basement's Melody Lounge, a randy patron had unscrewed one of the overhead lights in order to have more intimacy with his date. A bartender asked one of the

Grove's underpaid and underage busboys to replace the light. The Melody Lounge was dark and crowded, and the busboy lit a match in order to see the socket better. Immediately, one of the fake palm trees—bought on the cheap by Welansky—caught fire.

The only exit from the Melody Room was a four-foot-wide staircase leading up to the main floor; it was immediately crammed with people trying to escape the fire as it raced across the ceiling, igniting other furnishings and decorations in its wake. Employees tried in vain to kill the flames with water and seltzer bottles as patrons tried to escape through the door at the top of the stairs. Even though they eventually got it open, the crush of people against the doorway lodged people inside.

A fireball exploded into the main dining room, where guests were awaiting the start of the 10:00 p.m. show. Around one thousand people, crowded together around small chairs and tables before the bandstand, erupted into panic. Desperate to find an exit, many could locate only the single revolving door at the front of the Grove. While some escaped through back tunnels and windows, most were wedged into that revolving door, which got stuck as the fire raged throughout the Grove. An exit door in the newly built (but unlicensed) "New Lounge" provided some escape, but because the door swung inward, the rush of patrons swung the door shut, trapping even more people inside as massive heat, toxic gas, and fire consumed the atmosphere inside the Cocoanut Grove.

Many victims were brought to Mass General Hospital, where a triage center was set up in the lobby. Several floors above, Barney Welansky—proprietor of the Grove, who had nailed several doors shut and flouted safety protocols—convalesced, still recovering from his stroke. Reluctant attendee entertainer Buck Jones lingered at MGH for two more days before he, too, perished.

Later, officials discovered that the Grove had been given a "good" fire rating just a week before, a horrific irony considering that historians now believe the fire was at least exacerbated by a faulty air conditioning system that pumped highly flammable gas into the nightclub as the fire raged. This, in addition to shoddy repairs, cheap material, bad wiring, and those exit doors nailed shut, led to nearly five hundred deaths—more fatalities, incidentally, than the club's legal capacity. Welansky was eventually charged with nineteen counts of manslaughter on account of his gross negligence.

If there was a silver lining in the Grove's tragedy—the worst nightclub fire in America's history—it's that Massachusetts and states like it adopted new fire laws and safety protocols for venues. Now exits have to be clearly

Melody Lounge destroyed. *U.S. Army Signal Corps.*

marked and have outward-swinging doors, revolving doors must be accompanied by standard doors nearby, and highly flammable decorations are prohibited.

The New England Beachcomber locations soon changed. Joseph F. Dinneen of the *Boston Globe* reported in his "Spilling the Beans" column, "All of the night clubs open in Boston now bear the official stamp of approval of the city of Boston licensing and inspecting authorities and were certified as safe before they were permitted to resume business. Many of the places have been radically changed and no longer resemble their former selves. There are no artificial trees, no cloth decorations, no decorative fur, feathers, or tinsel." The article goes on to say that Boston artists were now decorating clubs with oil panels and that the "panels by Miron in the Beachcomber are exceptional." There's no mention of Tommy Maren's Boston Beachcomber past 1943.

Around 1945, the Beachcomber Lounge at the Graymore Hotel in Portland became the Arabian Lounge; whether proprietor S. William Richard just wanted a change in theming or was spooked by the Donn

Beach lawsuit, we may never know. Tiki—even proto-tiki—is hard to find in Maine, and it's a shame that we lost a venue like this one before the tiki era truly began.

As for Ruby Foo's Providence location, it hung on longer, even after removing some of the tropical décor. In 1950, the Crown Hotel was bought by new owners and remodeled the venue in accordance with the less extravagant aesthetic of the early 1950s. If only they'd held on just a little longer, the midcentury tiki explosion might have given the venue new and improved life.

The country was going through upheavals, and major changes were about to take hold coast to coast. Some of them would have a profound effect on the future of Polynesian pop, such as the advent of cheaper air travel, the Midcentury Modern design aesthetic, and the impending statehood of Hawai'i. But before all that, veterans of World War II would return home to find a country changed by sudden abundance, the new sprawl of suburbia, the rising teenage culture, and a newfound cultural desire for conformity.

They were going to need some way to escape.

Chapter 2

TIKI COMES EAST

*D*onn Beach may have been the first to employ the Polynesian pop concept in America, but he was certainly not the last—and wasn't necessarily the one to provide the most lasting impact on the States. Monte Proser had proven that imitation could be a key to success, but he had also proven that the imitation couldn't be blatant or so lacking in imagination. Enter Oakland, California's Vic Bergeron, who owned a small restaurant themed as a hunting lodge called Hinky Dinks. In 1937, he grew so inspired by Donn Beach's concept that he changed the style and name of his establishment and reopened as Trader Vic's. Bergeron's innovation was adding Chinese American food—which had grown popular in San Francisco during the Great Depression—to the menu and adapting it to his customers' tastes. His décor consisted of so-called exotic wares that he would often trade for food and drink, thus the name. When he expanded his business to San Francisco, he added one new crucial element to his restaurant: the Tiki.

Tiki comes from Māori mythology, meaning "the first man"; the more common *tiki*—in lowercase—signifies a carved humanoid figure, generally in wood or stone. The word crops up all over Polynesia, in the Cook Islands, Tuamotu, and the Marquesas Islands. In Tahitian, it's *ti'i*, and *ki'i* in Hawaiian. The various carvings can represent the original Tiki, other Polynesian gods, or ancestors who have been deified. When carvings and statuary eventually made it to the United States, quite often they were divorced from their religious and ancestral significance. They were added to establishments like Trader Vic's as another "authentic" artifact from a culture—actually, multiple cultures—that most mainland Americans hadn't experienced firsthand.

A perfect storm of events made the rise of Polynesian pop and American tiki (lowercase) culture seem almost inevitable. The bombing of Pearl Harbor in Hawai'i served as the catalyst to bring the United States into the war, tying Hawai'i—then an annexed territory serving as a strategic U.S. military base—closer to America than ever before. As World War II stormed the South Pacific, servicemen and women were getting their first taste of real Polynesia. Along with wartime trauma and (often undiagnosed) post-traumatic stress, these soldiers also brought back memories of island life—memories that grew romanticized the longer they were back in the States. In Jason Henderson and Adam Foshko's *California Tiki*, they discuss the novel and film *The Man in the Gray Flannel Suit*, which tackles the duality of men who had been forced to kill and who now were being forced to conform to suburban life, the atomic family, and the bland normalcy of office work. Being able to go to a Trader Vic's or Don the Beachcomber to escape into the fantasy and romance of the islands was a powerful draw.

The year 1947 brought those stories to life in the Pulitzer Prize–winning story collection by James Michener *Tales of the South Pacific*. Based on Michener's time as a navy man in the war, *Tales* introduced the fictional island of Bali Ha'i, a hazy, beautiful place on the horizon seemingly so close yet unattainable. Bali Ha'i stands as a totem for innocence, tranquility, and the American concept of what island life should be. Both Donn Beach and Trader Vic knew a little something about how to bring that concept to the mainland. A hugely successful Rodgers & Hammerstein musical followed, adding yet another unreal layer to the increasingly distant reality of war. Another book, *Kon-Tiki*, by Thor Heyerdahl, made a similarly major impact on Americans' desire for the exotic, charting the author's three-month journey from Peru to the island of Puka Puka on a balsa-wood raft. Heyerdahl's thesis supposed that an ancient American race settled the Polynesian islands accidentally via "drift voyaging," led by the mythical hero Kon-Tiki. While this was eventually disproven, the book's epic adventure on the open ocean grips readers now as it did in the late 1940s.

American culture was trending more conservative; the one-two-three punch of Prohibition, the Great Depression, and the war had taken its toll on the American psyche. Both New England's financial centers (particularly Boston) and its farming sectors suffered devastatingly during the Depression, and the Northeast states were sluggish to return to prosperity. The war helped the region in surprising ways: Massachusetts companies like Raytheon with its focus on electronics and Connecticut's aviation industries helped the war effort and buoyed the region's prospects. After the war, the nation utilized these hubs of education for defense of a different sort: protecting America in the Cold War. While Maine, Vermont, and New Hampshire lacked the resources of the lower states, their focus turned to the concept of leisure, vacation, and escape from the rat race of the cities. New England was America's atomic age in miniature—racing toward the future with massive advancements in technology, while creating spaces to hide from it all.

One of those spaces opened its doors to New England in 1955, the first "official" tiki establishment in the region. It came to us via the inventiveness of a man called Skipper Kent, one of the most unheralded figures in the early history of Polynesian pop. While Donn Beach and Vic Bergeron had been perfecting both their concepts and personas—the former, a beach bum; the latter, a sophisticated merchant and trader—in prewar California, Frank "Skipper" Kent was yachting around the world. He built his first yacht, the *Magic Carpet*, over the course of three years. With his wife, Lucille, Skipper sailed the globe, collecting artifacts and curios and rums that he would later utilize in his restaurants. In his second yacht, the *White Cloud*, Skipper sailed from Chicago to California and competed in yachting events like the Transpacific race from California to Honolulu in 1941 and 1947. From there, the world was his. Skipper loved sailing to exotic, romantic locales in the South Pacific, Australia, the Philippines, the West Indies, and the Caribbean. Through his travels, he became a rum expert, bringing that knowledge back to the States along with folk art and rare flora. He was particularly obsessed with orchids and built greenhouses on his home property in which to cultivate them for use in themed decoration. His first restaurant endeavor, The Skipper, opened in South Berkely in the late thirties, followed by Skipper Kent's Zombie Village, opened in 1942.

Despite its proximity to Don the Beachcomber, the Zombie Village didn't seem to draw Beach's ire like Monte Proser's wholesale copy-and-paste establishments on the East Coast did. (Speaking of proximity, Zombie Village opened across the street from the first Trader Vic's. Pre-tiki was already getting crowded in Southern California.) Kent not only debuted his own libations—including the South Sea Cooler and Pagan Love—but he also furthered the concept of what a Polynesian pop restaurant should be. Skipper was the one who innovated the colorful dangling glass floats, now a staple of tiki bar décor. He may also have invented the idea of the restaurant gift shop, selling wares from his travels all over the world, but Vic Bergeron might have gotten there first.

Polynesian Village Bar postcard. *Scott Schell.*

After feinting east with his Nevada bar, the evocatively named West Indies, Kent returned to California with his first eponymous restaurant. According to *Tiki Magazine and More*, Skipper Kent's in San Francisco had "one of the world's greatest collections of rums and liqueurs," befitting the authority for whom it was named. Still, the allure of the East—Rumifest Destiny?—called. Like Monte Proser and the prewar Beachcomber franchisees, Skipper Kent would partner with hotels to develop his brand-new restaurant concept: The Polynesian Village.

Testing the idea in Chicago's Edgewater Hotel first in 1954, the Skipper then brought the Polynesian Village to Boston's Somerset Hotel. The hotel already had a deep history in the region before tiki came to town. Opening just before the turn of the twentieth century, the Somerset was considered "among the distinctively magnificent hotels of the world," at least according to the *Boston Globe*. The hotel could back it up, though, with its giant marble staircase, gold and silver damask-paneled walls, and massive basement ballroom with columns of flawless Parian marble. During World War II, the hotel billeted navy soldiers who were studying at the Naval Academy at nearby Wentworth Institute. Still later, it would host The Beatles during the band's final tour in 1966 and house Red Sox player Ted Williams during the baseball season. In the midst of all, the Polynesian Village restaurant brought the breeze of the South Seas back to Beantown.

Immersive seems almost too subtle a word. Ken's wife, Lucille, his fellow adventurer and an accomplished painter in her own right, helped paint the dining rooms and banquet areas of both hotels, making the Polynesian Village a family affair. Beyond the paint, Skipper took the tenet of "no white walls" to electrifying extreme, covering each surface in rattan, tapa cloth, and decorated panels. Native masks, fearsome weapons, and Polynesian (or faux-Polynesian) art festooned these surfaces. Patrons could marvel at these treasures from their rattan or wicker peacock chairs, the latter of which felt elegantly thronelike in this adventurous setting. Everything was outlined in bamboo stalks, both as support and decoration, particularly over the alcove called the Kona Hut. A bamboo structure was draped with fish netting, inside which starfish had been snagged and now hung suspended over guests (a forerunner of the blowfish lamp?), and a hand-painted sign reading KONA HUT hung rakishly askew from one of the ceiling supports.

The nautical vibe predominated, with boat rigging and those somehow alluring glass floats hanging everywhere, but Kent didn't stray too far from Polynesian pop originalism. There were plenty of tikis everywhere, including a post behind the bar on which a tiki totem had been painted, and South Seas wall carvings hung under a thatched-roof booth just off the Kona Hut. A stolid-faced guardian stood sentry at the entry of the Kona Hut, whose carved wooden seriousness was undercut only by the pair of pink plastic leis it wore. If you're going to be the proprietor of an authentic tiki bar, by all means, treat the theme with purpose and reverence—but never forget the whimsy.

And all that is before we get to the drink menu. A marvel of Midcentury Modern design, this cream-and-melon-colored guide to libations featured an illustration of a yacht on the front, sailing through unknown tropical seas past palm trees and distant mountains. The thrillingly mod look continued inside, where sketches of beverages foregrounding those of distant oceans and warm, tropical shores bore the names of Kent's proprietary concoctions. The Tiger's Tooth boasted a "15-year-old Special Reserve Rum with lime juice," the Witch's Brew was "Just the thing the god Bacchus would order," and the Head Hunter, served in a fresh coconut, implored you to "take coconut home"! Polynesian Village's clientele was meant to feel not only that elusive feeling of escape but also the joys of indulgence. Kent's own history and bon vivant lifestyle informed much of the menu, with Skipper's Gold, the White Cloud (named for his yacht and featuring an ice cone; "How do we form the ice?" the menu asks, mysteriously), and Skipper Kent's Grog, which came with the alluring promise, "This one is masculine… Hmmm wonderful."

ISLAND
DRINK
FAVORITES

The

Polynesian

Village

SOMERSET HOTEL
BOSTON

SCORPION
Tropical punch with heavy
and light rums. Served in a
bowl to a group
3.25

SOUTH SEA COOLER
Cool and refreshing
Creme de Menthe blended
with rum
1.00

FOG CUTTER
You take the risk. One of
these and you can find your
way home in any fog
1.50

PAGAN BOWL
Served in a whole fresh
Hawaiian pineapple. A blend
of rum and pineapple
1.85

Polynesian Village menu. *Scott Schell.*

Widening our scope: the Midcentury aesthetic would grow to inform much of what would come to be known as the tenets of tiki. In architecture, minimalism, angular lines, basic geometrical shapes, and asymmetry would seem completely at odds with the so-called primitive aesthetics of tiki. But because Mid-Mod focused on minimalism and structural simplicity, it couldn't help but echo the simplicity-by-necessity of ancient architecture, which tended to use natural materials and basic forms. Look at the A-frame construction of traditional South Pacific meeting houses, seen in Palau and the Yap Islands, and maraes—tribal meeting houses—of New Zealand, which meshed somehow perfectly with Midcentury United States' fascination with sleek design. A-frame homes, cabins, and hotels became an atomic-age staple, rising to prominence simultaneously with the proliferation of A-frame tiki establishments. Frank Lloyd Wright's Prairie-style architecture, with its connected indoor and outdoor spaces, asymmetrical floor plans, and geometry, trickled down into Midcentury Modern architectural design and, from there, into the tiki subculture. From palm trees in porticos at Streamline Moderne airports to indoor waterfalls and bridges over streams inside tiki oases, the trends of the era seemed to inform each other and play off one another; futurism and "primitivism" were both exciting fantasies, providing new ways to break out of the humdrum (and sometimes stifling) present.

All of these ideas and elements would eventually make their way to one of the grandest tiki temples in the country, let alone New England. From small things, big things one day come: in 1950, Chinese immigrants Chun-Sau Chin and Tow See Chin opened Mandarin House, a small restaurant on Route 1 in Saugus, Massachusetts. The former ice cream parlor seated only about forty to fifty people and served Chinese and American dishes. There was no indication then what massive—literally *massive*—changes were in store, both for the restaurant and for Route 1 itself.

The Chins' daughter, Madeline, was born in Providence in 1927 and would eventually marry William Wong, whose own parents ran the popular Mai Fong restaurant in Boston. Together, the Wongs would buy out the Chins' interest in Mandarin House and, in 1958, change the name to Kowloon.

Mandarin House. *Kowloon Restaurant.*

Over the years and decades, the restaurant would expand and change to encompass all manner of Asian cuisines, its growth directly tied to the rise of the tiki trend in America—but it didn't start out that way. Bob Wong, one of Madeline and William's children, described the initial cuisine as a little more middle of the road: "When my grandparents ran it, it was chop suey and chow mein and a lot of American dishes, too, because American-born people weren't really familiar with Asian food....There was a lot of steak. Cutlets, pork chops, club sandwiches, BLTs, things like that. As people got a little more sophisticated with Chinese food, it grew."

Kowloon's shift from Chinese eatery to Polynesian paradise was a harbinger for the region. In 1951, restaurateur Tin Cheung Luke and his son Henry opened Luke's Chinese American Restaurant in Providence, Rhode Island. Occupying the space once inhabited by French restaurant Old France, Luke's didn't initially look remotely Chinese. Done in a rustic winter cabin décor, the simple tables were draped with checked tablecloths, and a stone country cabin fireplace dominated one wall, with a classic cathode-ray TV perched atop the mantel. The walls were done in knotty pine. Despite the surroundings, patrons, "considered Luke's to be the best, most authentic New York- and California-style Chinese food outside Boston." Pupu platters, beef skewers, lobster Cantonese, and chow mein were all on offer, the latter for only ninety cents a plate.

As tiki fever was beginning to grip the nation, Cheung Luke's son Henry decided to answer the moment, converting the upstairs area into a cocktail

Early days at the Kowloon. *Scott Schell.*

bar known as the Luau Hut. In contrast to the décor downstairs, the Luau Hut went full tiki—bamboo poles, rattan walls, and light fixtures that looked like giant clams. They served their Pina Paradise in a real pineapple and the Coco Kow in a fresh coconut and instilled a sense of urgency with their Rapa Virgin (presented in a coupe glass), declaiming, "The virgins of Rapa Island go mad without it!" Better have two!

The year 1951 was a fortuitous one for New England Chinese restaurants with Polynesian pop futures. Bob Lee's Lantern House opened in Boston's Chinatown, with only seven tables and serving standard Cantonese cuisine. The Aloha Cocktail Lounge debuted in early 1961, serving both classics like Mai Tais and Zombies but also double-named originals like the Hula Hula, the Pago Pago, and the Tiki Tiki. It was a harbinger of things to come. In an echo of what happened with Luke's, when Bob Lee's son took over the restaurant in the early 1960s, he leaned into the tiki trend hard, expanding and completely redoing the inside, renaming the restaurant Bob Lee's Islander.

Broken up into four areas—The Polynesian Room, the Hawaiian Room, the Luau Room, and the Aloha Cocktail Lounge—the rethemed Islander was anything but subtle. Polynesian décor festooned the place in every possible nook and cranny, starting with the high-contrast palm-patterned carpet and ending with the garish ceilings, boasting either an oversized floral print (Hawaiian Room) or a stylized tiki design, wild wavy lines in earth tones against a dark background (Polynesian Room). In between, your eye never got a chance to rest. Dozens of small carved tikis lined the wall between the ceiling and the thatched "roofs" over multiple seating areas, like a Polynesian frieze. Japanese lanterns suspended from the ceiling, casting a warm glow on both the tree-bark overhangs and the tiki totem poles around every corner. Those ubiquitous glass float lanterns dangled overhead, and you could gaze at painted panoramic island scenes—with sandy beaches, blameless blue skies, and an ocean that stretched into eternity—as if through a bamboo-framed window. More tiki idols of every size were scattered throughout, watching guests eat their "exotic Chinese foods" as they sat at long tables in rattan chairs in "the authentic Oriental seating arrangement," as one matchbook claimed.

Speaking of those "exotic Chinese foods": in the early 1980s, as the tiki trend was dwindling, The Islander declared in an advertisement, "We invented the pupu platter." The Hawaiian word *pū-pū* means "appetizer," and it was the only authentically Hawaiian thing about that delightful conglomeration of Chinese small bites. Usually including some combination of chicken fingers, pork strips, fried shrimp, chicken wings, and maybe beef teriyaki, the American pupu platter was often served in a wooden bowl with Sterno flames licking out of a hole in the top so to better resemble a volcano (of food?). In New England, it was often served with sticky-sweet duck sauce and, oddly, soft white dinner rolls, which you could butter and dunk into the duck sauce. Having been raised on Dunkin' Donuts, New Englanders love dunking stuff into other stuff.

In the realm of tiki, there are frequent legitimate discussions and arguments concerning progeny. Was it Trader Vic or Donn Beach who invented the Mai Tai, for example. Ditto the Zombie. But Lee's claim about the pupu platter is patently absurd. While The Islander had featured "Pu-Pu Platters heaped with shrimp puffs, fried won-ton, rumaki, barbecued spareribs, fried shrimp and barbecued chicken wings," according to a 1961 ad in the *Boston Record-American*, the Honolulu Trader Vic's listed a PuPu Platter on its menu in the 1950s, as did a number of other Hawaiian restaurants. (And rumaki—bacon-wrapped liver with water chestnuts soaked in soy sauce or brown sugar and then either fried or baked, neither Polynesian nor Chinese— was invented by Donn Beach. In early tiki, if you can't go authentic, make something up.)

So, while Bob Lee was many things— successful restaurateur and New England tiki innovator among them—he was not the inventor of the pupu platter.

Lee claimed that he'd come by this "Delightful Island Atmosphere" honestly. One promotional postcard read, "All tropical décor is authentic, collected during a 2-year search of the Islands by Host, Bob Lee, a man who has dedicated himself to the luxurious combination of the world's most valued pleasures, those of rare beauty and fine food." This postcard laid the atmosphere on as thick as that in the restaurant itself: "All who dream of far-off places…the romance of

Bob Lee's Islander matchbook. *Scott Schell.*

Tropical Gardens and rushing waterfalls…the mysterious mingling aromas of tropical foliage, native woods, and tropic streams…all who crave an atmosphere exciting, different, and wondrously beautiful, will realize the magnificence of a dream come true at Bob Lee's Islander."

Restaurants like Luke's, Bob Lee's, and Kowloon pointed toward an odd future of tiki in New England, particularly the Bay State. While these places went all in on the tiki trend, their later echoes didn't always feel a need to dive so deeply, and a trend toward less immersion and authenticity–whatever that means in this context–took hold in later years. James Teitelbaum in *Tiki Road Trip* marvels at this phenomenon, citing the "many, many Chinese joints with Tiki-inspired names that exist in Massachusetts. Why there is such an infestation of them here is anyone's guess." One guess: Chinese and Chinese American food exploded in popularity in the region due to the influence of restaurateur Joyce Chen, who changed the name of her dumplings to "Peking ravioli" to appeal to the Italian clientele at her Cambridge restaurant. She also pioneered mainstays of Chinese American eateries, like buffets that allowed dilettantes to sample the wares at their own pace and numbering the dishes to eliminate any orders getting lost in translation. Along with Ruby Foo, she became one of New England's first Asian American women to own and operate a restaurant empire.

Chinese American food, Caribbean-inspired libations, and Polynesian and Polynesian pop décor and architecture as the basic tenets of tiki were always strange bedfellows, a uniquely midcentury mainland American creation that reveled in the thrill of anything "exotic" to lift the country out of the undiscussed and unprocessed trauma following the war.

In New England, especially in Massachusetts, those tenuous connections stretched even further, attempting at times to make "Chinese" and "Polynesian" synonyms. While both the state and the region would go on to host many "authentically inauthentic" tiki and Polynesian pop venues, you can't discuss New England tiki without discussing the proliferation of these masquerading Chinese restaurants. Chef Jason Doo, owner of Wusong Road in Cambridge, Massachusetts, offered some clarity:

> *I actually spoke to my grandmother about this. On the East Coast, Chinese restaurants were actually "nice" restaurants when they first came up. There were date spots where you would go for something "exotic" and different. Most bartenders saw that tropical drinks were popular with Americans, so they reproduced them, adding to the "fun" aspect of the evening out. When a bunch of food comes out fast and drinks arrive in*

colorful cocktail mugs and glasses it always is a good way to break the awkward silence on a date. It gives you a common subject to talk about and a shared experience.

As the 1960s encroached, the tiki trend was poised to explode into all-out tiki fever, sweeping across the nation from its locus in Hollywood all the way over to the Atlantic Northeast. But maybe the biggest impact on Polynesian pop in America happened in 1959, when a bit of Polynesia actually *became* America. On August 21, 1959, Hawai'i joined the Union, and paradise had never seemed so close.

Chapter 3

TIKI FEVER

H awai'i's relationship to the United States had long been fraught. A history of westernization, cultural relativism, and imperialism culminated in the annexation of the Kingdom of Hawai'i in the late 1800s, making the island group both a part *of* America and apart *from* America. The 1915 Hawai'i pavilion at the Panama-Pacific International Exhibition stoked mainland fascination with Hawaiiana, and the *hapa haole* (pronounced "happa howlie," meaning part Hawaiian, part foreigner; in this case, signifying white performers approximating Hawaiian music) craze took off. The well-to-do had begun to travel to the islands by cruise ship, sailing on the luxurious Matson Line from California ports to Honolulu. A cheaper alternative to travel was the hugely popular radio show *Hawai'i Calls* (recorded in Hawai'i itself at the Moana Hotel! you could hear the sounds of the Waikiki surf as musicians performed live!). Debuting in 1935, it only further cemented the idea of Hawai'i being tied to America, while also being a far-off exotic place full of sounds and sights still foreign to most Americans.

After the attack on Pearl Harbor in 1941, the bond between the islands and the mainland seemed tighter than ever. As commercial air travel grew more affordable in the 1950s, more and more Americans could visit the islands, discovering that they were just as much a paradise as the travel brochures claimed. The national tension that existed between postwar victory and postwar trauma (not to mention the advent of the Cold War and the looming threat of nuclear catastrophe) made a place like Hawai'i seem necessary to the American psyche. Though we would do well to remember that Hawai'i, like any state, cannot be reduced to one concept or idea, the perception of sunny beaches and an ease of living so different from the rat race mentality of mainland America was entrancing. The well-timed publication of James Michener's new number-one novel, *Hawaii*, and Elvis Presley's Hawai'i movies and music only further sold the country on the land of palm trees and luaus being tantalizingly in reach.

One of the most interesting facets of this era of Hawai'i, especially as it relates to the tiki movement in America, is Oahu's Polynesian Cultural Center (PCC)—built, unusually, by the Church of Jesus Christ of Latter-day Saints (the LDS Church). The center had its roots in the tradition of the *hukilau*, a fishing festival in which all who participated would share in the catch. The term expanded in the early 1940s as the church threw a hukilau, complete with a luau and other Polynesian entertainment, as a fundraiser for a chapel that had been destroyed in a fire. Intended to preserve the understanding and traditions of the major Polynesian cultures—Hawai'i, Samoa, Aotearoa (New Zealand), Fiji, Tahiti, Tonga, and the Marquesas Islands, as well as Rapa Nui (Easter Island)—the PCC offered simulated tropical villages that featured performers displaying arts, crafts, music, and history of each culture. It was something like a Polynesian World's Fair.

By presenting simulations of real culture as seen through the eyes of observers of those cultures, the PCC was a harbinger for the larger tiki movement as it swept from the South Seas to California and eventually all the way to the East Coast. Despite some stabs at authenticity, many mainland tiki bars and restaurants would often simply merge these unique cultures in ways that looked most interesting or use them as jumping-off points for imagination and whimsy. If the Polynesian Cultural Center was a synecdoche of the South Pacific, Hawai'i and its statehood could serve the same purpose, especially in the eyes of their new American compatriots. If Polynesia was Hawai'i and Hawai'i was America, then maybe all of the South Seas was part of the melting pot of the United States, too—a sort of cultural manifest destiny.

Of course, not every American could afford air travel to our fiftieth state, and for those in far-flung New England, for whom California had always seemed so distant, Hawai'i was still not much more than a dream. Pop culture fueled the fire from coast to coast. Popular TV shows like *Hawaiian Eye* and *Hawaii 5-0* standardized what that dream should look like: sandy beaches, surfing, palm trees, and never-ending chill.

Those exotic thrills extended even to furniture and home living, because when America falls in love with a trend, it falls hard. Enter the Western International Trading Company, or, as people usually refer to it, Witco.

Let's take a step back for a moment. Designers of Midcentury Modern furniture often aimed for simplicity, functionality, and elegance. Creator George Nelson's simple Platform Bench—a long wooden slatted bench with rhomboid metal supports—was one of the first designs to kickstart the concept. It could be easily mass-produced and function everywhere, especially in communal places like office lobbies and bus stops. Designers Ray and Charles Eames thought of furniture and design as a democratic imperative, their philosophy being, "We want to make the best for the most for the least." Their Eames Lounge Chair, made entirely of plywood, with a gently curved seat and supportive back, is one of the most famous items of furniture in history. It was easy to manufacture, inexpensive to buy, and fun to sit in. Functional design without skimping on the whimsy. It's from designers like Nelson and the Eameses that we get the Mid-Mod aesthetics we think of today: the curving elegance of kidney and boomerang shapes; the geometry of spheres and squares that somehow don't seem contradictory; the use of wood, glass, metal, and plastic in excitingly simple, often organic-feeling pieces.

As tiki architecture developed in America concurrently with the new streamlined, *Jetsons*-style look that was popular with Midcentury diners, bowling alleys, and apartment buildings, so, too, did Witco grow contemporaneously with the Eames style. Founded in early 1958 by William Westerhaver, his cousin Robert Post Jr., and Robert Cookson, Witco started in the Pacific Northwest by importing art and carvings from Central and South America. Soon, though, Westerhaver wanted to start creating art himself in a similar style. Following a 1958 furniture and décor show in Los Angeles, Witco took off, both in conjunction with and separate from the surging popularity of Polynesian pop. Chunky sculptural art, tables, bars, chairs and couches, framed three-dimensional carvings you could hang on the wall like paintings—this was Witco's bread and butter. It, like tiki itself, was inspired by the look and feel of Oceania and South Pacific life, but its use of animal prints also gave it a "jungle" feel that was somewhat removed from the core of tiki. Elvis Presley's Jungle Room at Graceland was entirely filled with Witco work, from the furniture to the lamps to the carvings on the table.

Elvis became part of—and sometimes even came to define—the twin excitements of Hawaiiana and tiki, starring in three films about the new state (*Blue Hawaii*, *Girls Girls Girls*, and *Paradise, Hawaiian Style*) with accompanying Hawaiian-themed soundtracks. Rock-and-roll, Hawaiian style, was the sound of the now. Newer musical movements took over from the hapa haole craze of earlier decades to soundtrack this new era. Surf music—from instrumental guitar-based rock by the likes of Dick Dale and the Ventures to the surf-pop melodies of the Beach Boys—was active, buoyant, the perfect music to play on the beach or on the radio while hot-rodding. Mexican bandleader Esquivel was developing a type of music later defined as "Space Age Bachelor Pad Music," combining lounge music with elements of Latin and jazz.

Exotica music, a new version of lounge and jazz pioneered by the likes of Martin Denny and Les Baxter, offered haunting melodies played on instruments like the vibraphone, bongos, and the Japanese koto, and often accompanied by human-made animal sounds and bird calls—all of which was suitably strange enough to American ears to sound both new and primitive. In a way, it worked in the way many tiki bars did, by offering a sense of *elsewhere* without necessarily defining where that elsewhere was supposed to be.

Hawaiiana in all its forms only fueled the fire of the ongoing tiki craze and, in the melting-pot mentality of America, merged, modified, and recombined. Thus, surf music became, sort of, tiki music. Hot rods and car culture folded into the movement. Backyard luaus and home-based tiki bars became part of the American landscape. And the "real" thing? It exploded.

As California suddenly teemed with new tiki architecture—everything from apartment complexes to golf courses to bowling alleys now boasted the Polynesian pop vernacular—New England mainly contented itself with the likes of themed bars and restaurants…but not entirely. One of the exceptions was Seymour, Connecticut's Polynesian Motel—"Hawaii on the Housatonic!" Opening in 1959, the Polynesian opened along Route 34, a "frontage of 270 feet," with a small marina allowing patrons to visit by boat. The Polynesian boasted an indoor swimming pool—open, unusually, to the public but available for private luaus or "splash parties"—with steam rooms available for guests. The main dining room, simply called the Tiki Dining Room, might have been elaborately Polynesian for Connecticut, but the Asian lanterns hung from a stark white ceiling, the fake palms didn't quite convince anyone they were in the South Seas, and the tile floor betrayed the Tiki Dining Room for what it was: a banquet hall at a hotel. At least a raised dining area built from bamboo and thatch seemed to enhance the mood, and the huge and hideous frowning tiki at the entrance, with balloon-like cheeks and a hole at the top of his head (perfect, as shown in the official

BROTHER CLEVE

If one were to distill the many elements that define New England tiki into a single person, that person would be Brother Cleve. Born in Medford, Massachusetts, as Robert Toomey in 1955, Cleve was old enough to be aware of the first wave of American tiki without being a part of it. The punk scene in Boston called to him, and eventually he found himself frequenting Kenmore Square's infamous Rathskeller club, which hosted punk, hardcore, and pre-grunge rock bands like The Dead Kennedys, The Ramones, and the Pixies. Cleve toured with Boston-based garage band The Del Fuegos in the 1980s, which is when he got bitten by the cocktail bug. "I first got interested in classic cocktails in the mid-'80s; I was on tour....We were in this diner in Cleveland where the menu had a cocktail list with Sidecars, Grasshoppers, Ward Eights, etc. on it. I was fascinated and immediately went out and bought an Old Mr. Boston drink book."

Returning to Boston and the Rathskeller, Cleve found himself being offered a job as a bartender at the connected restaurant, James Ryan's Hoodoo Barbecue. Cleve immediately

Brother Cleve. *Gabriel Bascom.*

attempted to introduce classic cocktails to the denizens of Hoodoo and the Rat, but no one was drinking Manhattans or Sidecars in 1988. Within a few years, though, as the craft cocktail revolution had just begun making inroads, Combustible Edison came into Cleve's life and changed everything.

Punk wasn't Cleve's only musical obsession; he'd grown up fascinated with the lounge sounds of James Bond soundtracks and space age pop, later on citing bossa nova as his favorite cocktail music. As Cleve and many other punk kids started turning back to these vintage sounds, looking to both embrace and elevate the genre, Combustible Edison's neo-lounge came bundled with a whole happening in its arsenal. They played the type of music with which Cleve had once been so fascinated, but they were also into the lounge-era practice of crafting classy libations to go with their sound. They sold cocktail recipe books at shows and called their fans Cocktail Nation. When their keyboardist couldn't make a tour, they asked Brother Cleve to step in.

From there, Cleve went on to radically influence the local cocktail scene, guesting at bars and teaching the up-and-comers how to make classic drinks. He designed drink menus for local bars and created the first weekly lounge music and cocktail party—he called it Saturnalia—at the Lizard Lounge in Cambridge. He did a stint at Patrick Sullivan's influential B-Sides Lounge in Cambridge, Massachusetts, teaching and inspiring a generation of bartenders and mixologists. In 2007, *DrinkBoston* ran a profile on him, stating, "Not to get all hyperbolic, but the contemporary Boston cocktail scene as we know it wouldn't exist without him." Everyone in the community roundly agreed.

Cleve became a scene unto himself. He was a member of the wildly satirical Church of the SubGenius. He worked with Esquivel, writing liner notes for new records and reissues of the bandleader's classic albums. Cleve would tour everywhere, teaching seminars on the history of the Zombie and the Mai

Tai, embracing the tiki renaissance, DJing classic exotica and surf and bossa nova records. When a bar or a gathering needed an expert mixologist, musicologist, or historian versed in New England cocktails and bars, they called on Brother Cleve. When the newly formed New England Tiki Society needed a DJ for their events, they called on Brother Cleve. When the author of this book needed to know specifics about the history of New England tiki bars, I called on Brother Cleve. He told me everything I needed to know and then gave me a list of must-have exotica albums, just for my edification.

When Cleve died suddenly in late 2022, he had just appeared at Tiki by the Sea, an educational event in Los Angeles. Teaching and influencing new generations about tiki, cocktail, lounge, and exotica was his whole ethos. When he told you a story, you wanted to grab a Mai Tai and settle in; his tales were always long and discursive, but they were always compelling.

In October 2022, the New England Tiki Society threw a fundraiser for Cleve's wife, Diane, at Wusong Road in Cambridge, Massachusetts. It was not the only fundraiser for Cleve—he touched a lot of people—but it was the one I attended. The "Le Mai Tai" fountain. The friends from all corners of Cleve's life. The slideshow playing scenes of Cleve throughout his life. The playlist soundtracking the night, which had been curated by Cleve himself. All reasons to remember what a world he'd created around himself and why, when we raised a shot of rum to him and called out his name, there wasn't a dry eye in the place.

New England tiki would be in a different, likely poorer and shabbier place without the guiding influence of Brother Cleve. This book could not have been written without him. I didn't get nearly as much time with him as I could have wanted, but I will forever cherish his readiness to guide me, his immediate kindness and generosity, and that smile when I handed him another craft cocktail at Wusong Road. He really loved a well-made cocktail.

postcard, for sticking a cocktail umbrella in), preserved at least a semblance of tiki immersion.

Connecticut wouldn't have to wait much longer for a far more authentic Polynesian pop experience. The South Seas, which came to both Hartford and New Haven in the 1960s, had its origins in late 1950s Massachusetts. Originating in Boston's Chinatown under the supervision of World War II vet and prolific restaurateur Henry Oi, the South Seas has the distinction of being New England's first homegrown tiki chain. Interestingly, while the menu boasted Luau Dinners ("The Islands' Special Feast") which were essentially varying sizes of pupu platters, and "Flaming Ambrosias" (standard American fare like steak, duck, chicken, or lobster, spiced up with pineapple chunks in sauce for that South Pacific flavor), they didn't really push their cocktail selection with any particular flair. There were tiki drinks on offer—you could get a Zombie, a Singapore Sling, a Cuba Libre—but they were simply listed among the other cocktails and "tall drinks." For a venue that went all in on décor, the mainstay of tropical drinks just blended into the background.

But wow, that décor. The 1961 opening of the Hartford location elicited a rapturous review from the Sunday *Herald*: "The new restaurant … will feature the same exciting dishes and exotic beverages which have made Boston's South Seas famous. Particularly interesting will be the Luaus, or Hawaiian

The Polynesian, Seymour, Connecticut. *Scott Schell.*

Betty Oi, Tom Wong, and Janet Wong, of the Hawaiian. *Scott Schell.*

feasts, which will be introduced to the area. The main dining room has an intimate island atmosphere....The main prop is a cleverly designed waterfall which trickles into a pool containing tropical plants and creatures of the islands....Tropical palms, fishnets, and other supports further authenticate the atmosphere." The article concluded, "So real was the atmosphere that the sarong and the grass skirt would not have been out of place should the well-wishers [the invited guests] chosen to wear them."

Henry Oi was big on that feel of authenticity at his restaurants, which also included The Hawaiian—opened in 1964 on Boylston Street in Boston, managed by Tom Wong—whose Waikiki Lounge promised "Island Entertainment." So enthralled was Oi with Hawaiian theming that he went direct to the source for his South Seas Boston location, purchasing two immense tiki statues direct from the fiftieth state, both carved out of royal Hawaiian palm wood and representing male and female deities. While the male statue was firmly ensconced in the dining room, the female had been left unprotected in the foyer of the restaurant. The *Boston Globe* put what happened next in colorful context: "Some lowlife sneaked a 300-pound six-foot statue of a Polynesian goddess out of the South Seas Restaurant....She is the goddess of love, food, and prosperity—and how can you beat that combination." Oi circulated a picture of one of South Seas' waitresses, Mae Chin, standing beside the male statue, with an attached note begging to be contacted about the whereabouts of the missing statue. As far as I know, it was never recovered.

Speaking of tiki franchises, we now come to the curious case of the name Hu Ke Lau and the tangled history of the many restaurants who bore it. When it comes to tiki restaurants, some names are just too good to let a single proprietor have it all to themselves. Across the country, any number of Bamboo Huts (two in Massachusetts alone!) or Oriental Gardens or Polynesian Villages abounded, and not even Florida's legendary Mai-Kai was safe (as we'll see in the following decades, as Peter Yee's New Hampshire restaurant empire multiplied). But the name Hu Ke Lau is especially thorny, the history a little murky, and not all restaurants were created the same.

We know that the Chicopee, Massachusetts location opened in 1965 and for a long time was a true tiki temple. It was festooned with carvings in every corner and free bit of floor space, some in alcoves lit from behind for the most dramatic effect. Large Hawaiian murals dominated entire walls, and the booths were small huts surrounded by thick bamboo poles lashed together by rope. Pointed roofs offered the feeling of private seating, even in the large open dining area. Water features and aquariums abounded, banyan trees proliferated, and the long front of the restaurant was dominated by a simple painted mural with plastic 3-D palm fronds at intervals. A small A-frame stood over the door, and a tiki mask peered out from within its triangle, glowing from within as day turned to dusk. A long-running Polynesian dance and dinner show started up near the end of the 1960s and continued performing all the way up until the venue's closing.

(The Polynesian influence on Chicopee isn't just limited to the Hu Ke Lau, interestingly. Just off nearby Maui Drive, we find both Tiki Circle and Kon Tiki Circle, surrounding the mobile homes of Kon-Tiki Village. There's no evidence of tiki architecture here, but it's tantalizingly strange that this small town in Massachusetts has a little area inspired—at least in name—by the far-off South Pacific.)

But Chicopee is not the last word in Hu Ke Laus, even though it might have been the first.

Co-owner Bobby Lew celebrated the openings of the Longmeadow and Pittsfield, Massachusetts locations in 1969, and in the 1970s, he branched

Mae Chin with Tiki, South Seas, Connecticut. *Scott Schell.*

out to Connecticut with locations in Rocky Hill and West Hartford. In the mid-1970s, he and his co-owners sold the Longmeadow location, allowing the new owners to retain the name—a name that was growing beyond even Bobby Lew's influence. New unaffiliated Connecticut locations opened in Bridgeport and Bloomfield Center, not to mention one in Manchester, New Hampshire, and in 1972, a Hu Ke Lau made its debut in South Portland, Maine ("Maine's No. 1 Chinese & American Restaurant" read one ad, featuring line art of a wide-eyed tiki and a gardenia, "Behind Sears").

The South Portland Hu Ke Lau has a distinctly New England–Polynesian provenance. Chan-Sun Ng, who went by "Sonny," immigrated to the United States from China in the late 1940s, when he was still a boy. In 1963, he moved to Maine and found work in Portland's Pagoda restaurant. That same year, the Dunfey family of hoteliers opened the Hawaiian Hut as part of the Eastland Motor Hotel. It was Maine's first hardcore tiki establishment. "*Nui puka!*" (Grand Opening!) one ad in the *Portland Press Herald* cried. "The Dunfey family urges you to ho'o kipa mai—'Come and be friendly'—at the nui puka of the excitingly different Hawaiian Hut." For the time and place, the Hut really was excitingly different, with Pele Tiki and Her Island Revue promising "Exciting, Primitive Dances" onstage three times a night. You could dance to the wild sounds in the Hut's Coral Room. All around were Maine's first real brushes with the world of tiki. Bamboo and thatch, tapa cloth and Hawaiian luaus (in the form of buffets Tuesday through Thursday)—the Dunfey family went all in on Pacific theater. The menu came in the shape of a grass hut, with both classic Polynesian pop cocktails—your Zombie, your Mai Tai, your Dr. Funk—and hilarious Hawaiian Hut originals like Abel Mabel and Honorable Dave (described as "a treat that Dave suggests—a real stinker"; who Dave is remains a mystery).

It was into this environment that Sonny Ng arrived as a cook, leaving the Pagoda behind. He stayed on, eventually marrying the Hut's hostess and fathering a son named Bobby. Several years later, Sonny left the hut to start his own business: South Portland's own Hu Ke Lau restaurant. Though in no way connected to the rest of the New England Hu Ke Laus, Portland's distinguished itself through a quiet tiki and Chinese American legacy; Sonny Ng, his second wife, and all his sons worked at the Hu Ke Lau before it finally closed in 1994—four years later than the Hawaiian Hut he'd left behind.

Time and circumstance were not always kind to the New England Hu Ke Laus; in 1972, Bobby Lew was arrested for health code violations at the Rocky Hill location. It remained open until 1986, so presumably he cleaned up his act. Not so for the Bridgeport location, which was opened in 1980 by Arthur "Tilly" Russo and Vincent Curcio. Bridgeport was a bit of a sketchy place to be in the early 1980s. "This city is filled with the mafia," one Bridgeportian said at the time. Another elaborated, "You got scary hoods and spooky FBI agents all over the place." A waitress at the Hu Ke Lau lamented, "My friends think I'm nuts to work here. They say that when men come bursting through that door with shotguns, I'd better drop to the floor fast and play dead."

TIKI IS THE BEGINNING . . .
KEENTIKI'S THE LIVING END!
An exotic Polynesian paradise, right here
in New Hampshire. Visit this timeless world
of South Seas Enchantment. Dine on famed
Cantonese dishes, and refresh yourself with
a cool island drink. Visit New Hampshire's
unique Keentiki.

KEENTIKI
45 MAIN STREET, KEENE, NEW HAMPSHIRE
At The Crossroads of the Monadnock Region

Keentiki ad. *Scott Schell.*

Her friends were right. In 1981, federal agents raided the Bridgeport Hu Ke Lau, finding vast stores of cocaine, weapons, and illicit cash. Whether coincidentally or not, the establishment burned down in 1983 after it changed owners. Years after the tragic fire at the Cocoanut Grove, tropical locales sometimes had a way of burning down. Such was the fate that befell the uniquely named Keentiki, a 1966 restaurant in Keene, New Hampshire, that occupied the space left by the long-lived but departing Bon Ton Restaurant. An ad for the new establishment capitalized on '60s slang for its come-on: "Tiki's the beginning…Keentiki's the living end!" Very little is known about Keentiki beyond the ads ("The promise of Eastern graciousness…rare ancient recipes…Luxurious Polynesian atmosphere"), the fact that the old BON TON name was hidden within the block letters of KEENTIKI whenever it appeared in print—and that it was gutted by fire in 1967, just a year after its debut. The living end, indeed.

Even without the sudden devastation of fire, one by one, the New England Hu Ke Laus closed their doors, as tiki fell out of favor and the '60s gave way to the '70s and '80s. The Lenox location sold and became the Luau Hale in 1974 and still exists under that name, clinging to some classic tiki atmosphere with painted tropical murals and occasional tikis and water features. Only two Hu Ke Laus managed to make it to the new millennium. The Longmeadow location, long devoid of real tiki flavor or flair, shuttered its doors in 2016. But the original, still as tiki as Chicopee got while giving into modern intrusions like scratch ticket machines and TVs above the bar, held out until 2018. One of the heartbreaks of immersing yourself in the world of tiki is the simple fact that restaurants and bars tend to close, leaving both the patrons and the proprietors with only memories. On the occasion of its closing, Hu Ke Lau owner Andy Yee promised a new Hu Ke Lau in the same location, stating, "We're here for the long haul." However, five years later, no new Chicopee Hu Ke Lau has emerged. The odd legacy of Hu Ke Lau seems to have ended in New England.

It is here we turn our sights to Peter Yee, who came a little late to the tiki game but made up for it with such ambition and enthusiasm that he really deserves a place in the pantheon of New England's Polynesian pop

Hu Ke Lau postcard. *Author's collection.*

movement. In 1972, as tiki was falling out of favor on the West Coast, Yee opened the Tiki Lau in Westford, Massachusetts. The brick building was fronted by…well, it wasn't an A-frame so much as a Colonial-style peaked roof with standard asphalt shingles. However, an imposing *moai* with glowing eyes peered out from beneath it, and twin columns of molded glass blocks set into the bricks gave this very New England edifice an understated Midcentury feel. The tiki feel wasn't all that immersive within, though a fountain at the entrance, occasional tikis, and a bamboo-rich bar area gave it a passing grade. A second location in Amesbury, Massachusetts, opened soon after.

Where Yee's empire really took hold was in New Hampshire. In 1974, he opened the Mai Kai in Manchester. Naming his tiki restaurant Mai Kai was already flirting with disaster; the palatial tiki temple of the same name in Fort Lauderdale, Florida, is one of the best and most revered in the world. But Yee did everything possible to make the comparison a favorable one, decking out his Manchester location with immense tiki carvings, mounted spears and shields, and painted murals of tropical sunsets and active volcanoes spread across full walls. The outer A-frame was fairly immense, jutting out at an

Mai Kai, Manchester, New Hampshire. *Scott Schell.*

angle (unlike the incongruous symmetry of the Tiki Lau's attempt), a carved tiki within that would be illuminated at night. It was a restaurant worthy of being called the Mai Kai.

Not content with one location, however, Yee expanded across New Hampshire, opening new Mai Kais into the 1980s in Concord, Dover, and Hampton Beach. He ran into a little trouble with the law in 1986, but unlike the tiki restaurants that burned down or were found with piles of cocaine in their back rooms, Yee's more mundane crime involved copyright infringement. His restaurants were playing music that they weren't cleared for, a violation for which Yee got in trouble more than once. With the somewhat tumultuous history of tiki restaurants, it seems more than a little amusing that a restaurant would get in trouble for playing Bruce Springsteen's "Dancing in the Dark" without proper licensing, but it's one of the stories that make up the grand tapestry of Northeast tiki.

Homegrown chains weren't the only ones making inroads in New England. Here we return to our intrepid world traveler Skipper Kent, who had made such a go of it with the Polynesian Village in the Somerset Hotel. Kent's newest venture again involved pairing Polynesia with hotels, but his plans this time were a little grander in scope. Not just *a* hotel, but a hotel *chain*, in this case the Sheraton brand—one of the biggest names in hospitality, who were eager to compete with Trader Vic's partnership with Hilton Hotels. In the late 1950s, Skipper Kent worked with Sheraton to develop a plan for a series of restaurants in Sheratons across North America—and then decided to move to Hawai'i and pass out of this story forever.

Before he left, however, he put a worthy successor in his place: Stephen Crane, one of the most important people in the history of tiki. While most tikiphiles remember Donn Beach and Vic Bergeron and think of Skipper

Kent—if at all—as a blip on the scene, most forget about Crane entirely. Like the other three, Crane staked his claim in Hollywood; unlike them, Crane was *of* Hollywood, as a part-time actor and onetime husband to glamorous A-lister Lana Turner. Crane's initial claim to tiki fame was purchasing the pre-tiki Beverly Hills restaurant The Tropics and in 1953, transforming it into The Luau, a full-on Polynesian pop showplace. He emphasized the Polynesian gods in a way Beach, Bergeron, and Skipper Kent never had; it wouldn't be overstating it to say that the world would never have had the tiki scene that it had without Stephen Crane.

Crane's partnership with Sheraton Hotels began in 1958, taking the form of the Kon-Tiki chain, named for the book by Thor Heyerdahl, one of the most recognizable titles in Polynesian pop culture. Kon-Tiki restaurants opened rapidly in Montreal, Cleveland, Cincinnati, back to the locus of tiki in Waikiki, and on the mainland in Portland, Oregon. All hewed close to the tenets of classic Polynesian pop restaurants, rich with theme and overstuffed with atmosphere. Water features, native art, fishing floats, giant clam shells, and, of course, tikis all abounded. After so many successful ventures with this initial concept, Crane wanted to try his hand at a spinoff. And he set his sights on Boston.

The new venture was called Kon-Tiki Ports, a dining experience that would feature a series of rooms, each themed to a specific "exotic" port of call—as if one was traveling the world by raft and touching down in these far-flung places for a bit of food and grog. Each room of this new restaurant was richly decorated in the style of the port for which it was named: Papeete, Macao, Saigon, Singapore Joe's, and Bangkok. While similar locations opened in Chicago and Dallas (the latter of which was called simply Ports O'Call), only Boston's Sheraton, located in the city's Back Bay region in the sprawling mall known as the Prudential Center, got the Bangkok Room. A sumptuous area dominated by reds and golds, the Bangkok Room featured Thai-inspired statues, an inside verandah with grand columns and table seating, and an enormous fountain in the middle of the room. Not much reflected traditional Thai architecture, and none of it really has anything to do with tiki, but it was still exciting for Boston to have an exclusive claim on this little slice of faux Southeast Asia.

The Papeete room, the closest to what Crane had been known for with his Kon-Tiki restaurants, was described as such on postcards: "Nature has been tamed for this tropic hideaway. A waterfall babbles for your pleasure while local wildlife stands motionless to keep you at ease. But spears and pelts remind the diner that the simple life does have its excitements."

Monte Proser's Home of the Zombie postcard. *Scott Schell.*

Ruby Foo's Beachcomber postcard. *Scott Schell.*

Left: The Tropical Room. *Scott Schell.*

Below: Aku Aku postcard. *Scott Schell.*

Bamboo Hut postcard. *Scott Schell.*

Diamond Head dance floor. *Scott Schell.*

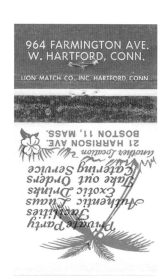

964 FARMINGTON AVE.
W. HARTFORD, CONN.

LION MATCH CO., INC. HARTFORD, CONN.

21 HARRISON AVE.
BOSTON 11, MASS.

Another location
Catering Service
Take out Orders
Exotic Drinks
Authentic Luaus
Facilities
Private Party

TEL. 233-9851

SOUTH SEAS

RESTAURANT
Lounge

STRIKE ON BACK COVER

Left: South Seas matchbook. *Scott Schell.*

Below: Beachcomber Lounge, Bonnie Oaks postcard. *Author's collection.*

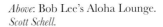

LION MATCH CORP. OF AMERICA - BOSTON

Above: Bob Lee's Aloha Lounge. *Scott Schell.*

Left: Bob Lee's matchbook. *Scott Schell.*

Scorpion Bowl
Planters Punch
Head Hunter
Love Potion   Zombie
Hula Hula   Mai Tai
Pineapple Passion
Bob's Aloha Delight

Aloha Lounge
Islander and

BOB LEE'S

LIBERTY 2-3997
OPEN 11a.m. to 3a.m.

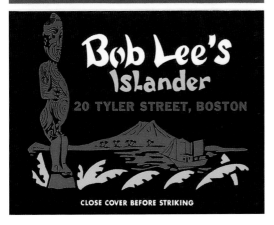

Bob Lee's
Islander
20 TYLER STREET, BOSTON

CLOSE COVER BEFORE STRIKING

Kona Hut at the Polynesian Village. *Scott Schell.*

Polynesian Village. *Scott Schell.*

Above: Polynesian Village. *Scott Schell.*

Left: Polynesian Village matchbook. *Scott Schell.*

Bamboo Hut. *Scott Schell.*

Bob Lee's Lantern House. *Scott Schell.*

The Hawaiian postcard. *Scott Schell.*

Bob Lee's Islander. *Scott Schell.*

Left: The Islander matchbook. *Scott Schell.*

Below: Honolulu. *Scott Schell.*

Left: South Pacific matchbook. *Scott Schell.*

Above: South Seas menu. *Scott Schell.*

Kowloon postcard. *Scott Schell.*

South Seas, Connecticut. *Scott Schell.*

Bob Lee's Islander. *Scott Schell.*

Wusong Road second floor. *Gabriel Bascom.*

New England Tiki Society at Kowloon. *Gabriel Bascom.*

Gabriel Bascom. *Gabriel Bascom.*

Left: Hawaiian Kū at Peabody Essex Museum. *Gabriel Bascom.*

Below: Kowloon at night. *Kevin Quigley.*

Above: Kevin Quigley and Xtine Benoit at a New England Tiki Society meet-up. *Gabriel Bascom.*

Left: Mug shelf at Wusong Road. *Kevin Quigley.*

Right: Kon-Tiki Ports ad. *Author's collection.*

Below: Kon-Tiki Ports postcard. *Scott Schell.*

The rooms were each meticulously appointed, hewing as close to the region it represented as possible in this restaurant setting. The Saigon Room was all reds and whites and golds, leaning heavily on Chinese influence, with a pagoda feel and a fountain in the center of the room. Singapore Joe's was a, uh, celebration of British imperialism, with "your table—once the hatch cover of a ship that once proudly carried Her Majesty's flag to far-flung harbors." The room, somewhat unnervingly authentic, boasted Asian influences overlain with UK flags draped from above. But the Papeete Room was exactly in line with what Crane had brought to his original Luau and Kon-Tiki restaurants, packed with carved tiki poles and a thatch roof with bamboo supports, from which Japanese fish floats, glowing pufferfish, and lanterns wrapped in tapa cloth dangled. The exotic vegetation and alluring décor were a far cry from the hustle and bustle of mid-'60s Boylston and Newbury Streets, just a few blocks away.

One must note the menus here, because they were among the restaurants' most appealing aspects. Instead of illustrations of beverages like many tiki restaurants, Kon-Tiki and Kon-Tiki Ports featured a photographic spread of exotic libations in the containers they would be served in: tiki mugs with garish faces, highball glasses and snifters filled to the top with colorful grog, and real pineapples clustered on a sandy shore before a distant tropical backdrop, serenely promising endless dusk. Crane's establishments were all about the garnish game, too, with intricate ice mounds, novelty backscratchers, and flaming lime wedges floating like tiny volcanoes on top of your cocktail. As with the best tiki, theatrics and presentation were everything, and the Kon-Tiki Ports' sense of exotic illusion was on point. A Sheraton ad proclaimed, "The exotic South Seas are in the Back Bay," and it wasn't lying.

Not to be outdone, Trader Vic's finally came to New England the same year, 1965, when tiki was at its most culturally saturated and Boston could sustain three major Polynesian locations (including the still-thriving Polynesian Room at the Somerset). In fact, one article claimed that this, the fifteenth Trader Vic's establishment, would be the franchise's largest. Located in the Statler Hilton on Arlington Street, Boston's Trader Vic's was something of a minor phenomenon—not necessarily because of its décor or cocktail menu but, unusually for a tiki restaurant, for its food.

"Certainly one of the 10 best in the city," claimed *Boston Globe*'s food critic Anthony Spinazzola, nearly a decade after he had declared it "one of Boston's most underrated eating places." Going out of his way to praise the restaurant's Continental/Polynesian fare, Spinazzola praised the lamb curry, the beef stroganoff, and the Cornish game hen and went into paroxysms of joy

Trader Vic's Boston. *Scott Schell.*

describing the "special lobster": "a truly superb location." Indeed, many of the ads touting the restaurant were careful to explain what the restaurant served ("What Is a Trader Vic's?" asked one ad, before listing the Hong Kong Steak, Indian Curries, and of course the Lobster Trader Vic's) and underscored in other ads that "Yes You Can Get American Food at Trader Vic's." It seems, in hindsight, a strangely vehement campaign designed to assure Bostonians about the potential unknown of pseudo-Polynesian foods; after all, hadn't the city, already home to a thriving Chinatown, gotten used to so-called exotic flavors?

In many ways, Boston's Trader Vic's was similar to the others across the country, with its pair of giant Chinese ovens, tapa cloth, starfish in nets, and the same sorts of weapons the Papeete Room at Kon-Tiki Ports boasted displayed on its walls. A trio of giant outrigger canoes dangled from the ceiling, measuring between ten and sixteen feet each, while small Guinea masks looked on with unblinking eyes, and giant sharks' jaws hung menacingly, having long lost the ambition to bite.

These were national chains, spinning out from some of the West Coast's tiki originalists. (The only one missing, Don the Beachcomber, never strayed farther east than Minnesota—give or take a jaunt across the Atlantic. The sixteen locations mainly clustered in California and Hawaii, with some one-offs in places like Texas in Nevada and, strangely, a couple in London. Why settle for *New* England when you can have *Old?*) The tiki trend was so pervasive in America that the Northeast states were no longer immune to its immersion. That these classic establishments could gain a toehold in far-flung New England (whose own nautical past and—truth be told—its own problematic history with the natives of its region echo America's history in the Pacific) seemed to prove that tiki was here to stay.

And while there was some truth to that, at least in New England, trends have a way of mutating and shifting away from their platonic ideal. How much longer would this version of tiki—robustly imagined, authentically inauthentic, multi-room paeans to long-dead and somewhat fictitious tiki gods—last?

Well, that depends on what route you took.

Chapter 4

WE'LL ALWAYS HAVE KOWLOON

Route 1 in Saugus and Lynnfield is New England's answer to the pop architectural style known as California Crazy. Also known as "programmatic architecture," California Crazy buildings mimicked what was sold inside, blown up to giant proportions. Thus, The Donut Hole in La Puente was a drive-through building in the shape of a donut, its name curving over the arch of the hole that you actually drove through; the Big Red Piano Shop was in the shape of, literally, a big red piano. The vernacular adapted so that the Brown Derby Restaurant could be in the shape of a gigantic brown derby and the Parasol Restaurant could approximate a humongous parasol above its diners' heads.

Not to be outdone, the thrillingly tacky, oversized gallery of buildings and structures along Route 1 was (and still is) particularly bizarre out here in the Atlantic Northeast. We're used to stately, serious Colonial buildings, humble Cape Cod homes, and the occasional Victorian mansion with old-world cupulas and widows' walks. What we don't expect is a giant orange dinosaur with bulging eyes, grinning inexplicably from a mini golf course on a hill. Nor do we expect a huge Leaning Tower of Pizza (Prince Pizzeria), a massive Chinese palace up on a hill that was so big it needed escalators (Weylu's), or a steakhouse that was so enamored of its western theme that it was represented by a positively gargantuan neon cactus out front that you could see for miles. But Route 1 got those things and more, including three Polynesian pop palaces that helped make Route 1 the magically transcendent and astonishingly kitschy place that lives squarely in many a New Englander's nostalgia.

Over the course of the 1960s and early 1970s, Kowloon slowly expanded, on its way to assuming its enormous final form. Around 1960, after the restaurant changed its name from Mandarin House, it added its first expansion, and there was a side entrance to the Peninsula Cocktail Lounge. Sunken interiors were becoming the rage, and just as cast members on *The Dick Van Dyke Show* and *The Mary Tyler Moore Show* had to step down into their impractically dipped living rooms, so, too, did patrons at the Peninsula Cocktail Lounge. Along with the carved tikis, the multiple water features, and the large tropical mural whose waterfall appeared to flow (thanks to hidden light projections), the sunken lounge offered something architecturally exotic. Before Kowloon's full growth spurt, having a lounge you had to step down into made the place seem larger, giving the eye something even more dramatic to settle on. Remember: tiki bars and restaurants are concerned with spectacle and theatricality; anything to distinguish them from the myriad other similar places is worthy.

The extensive cocktail menu, like that of the Kon-Tiki Ports, showcased the many beverages in pictures rather than in illustrations, and in the 1960s, their garnish game was just as on point. There was the Kowloon Gold (an interpretation of the Gold Cup, invented at the Captain's Inn in Long Beach, California), which utilized the ice shell, a molded miniature bowl of ice rising perpendicular from the liquid. The Marina Grog featured the similarly molded ice cone, while the Mai Tai and the Deep Sea Diver were topped with gardens of gardenias and mint. Their Boo-Loo was served in a whole pineapple.

In the early 1970s, Kowloon added a second-floor function room (to later serve as a popular stand-up venue starting in the 1990s) and soon constructed their Volcano Room, where the mural of an island volcano is in a constant state of eruption and where you could get the Kowloon version of a Scorpion Bowl—the Volcano Bowl. And this is when Kowloon attained its most famous landmark, the icon for which it became known, its entry into the pantheon of gigantic Route 1 oddities and excitements: the monolithic Hawaiian Kū carving and the A-frame under which it stood sentry.

The immense Kū god came direct from a tiki/tropical retailer and supplier known as Oceanic Arts, out of Whittier, California, an operation with its own rich history. Begun in 1956 by the team of LeRoy Schmaltz and Robert Van Oosting, Oceanic Arts became the premier destination for all your tiki needs. They supplied carvings, lamps, giant seashells, signs, and

Kowloon postcard. *Scott Schell.*

more for tiki and tropical destinations all around the world. They carved the tikis for the Enchanted Tiki Room in Disneyland and the bespoke wooden signs at the Polynesian Village Resort in Walt Disney World. They supplied many of the classic tiki bars and restaurants discussed in this book, including Don the Beachcomber, Trader Vic's, and Kon-Tiki Ports. They were one of the most respected names in Polynesian pop and American tiki culture, building and maintaining their business with integrity and almost supernatural levels of talent.

While they imported many of their wares for use in tiki destinations, one of their biggest claims to fame was their carvings. The team visited and studied the local arts and cultures of the islands they worked to represent on the mainland, aiming for authenticity whenever possible. Schmaltz was a master carver, working in the vein of the actual island nations of the South Pacific; thus, a Tahitian-style carving would seem Tahitian, and work representing Samoa would have the look and feel of authentic Samoan art. Diversity and equity in their interpretations of the distinct nations of the South Seas were immensely important to the folks at OA.

As Oceanic Arts grew, Van Oosting and Schmaltz employed many brilliant carvers and artists who helped define the shop as the premier location for tiki, Polynesian pop, and tropical supplies. But it was Schmaltz himself

Diamond Head menu. *Scott Schell.*

who carved the giant Hawaiian Kū that came to symbolize Kowloon restaurant, a benevolent totem overseeing Route 1 for decades.

Oceanic Arts closed its doors in 2021, and LeRoy Schmaltz sadly died soon after, but his and the rest of OA's artwork live on in the work and the art they created for the world of American tiki since the midcentury. There was a reason they were known as the Godfathers of Tiki.

During Oceanic Arts' heyday, even New England could support more than one Saugus-born, Hawaii-inspired restaurant. Not content to let a single tiki restaurant assume complete dominance over Route 1, Diamond Head opened in 1968, with its own classic A-frame under which a tiki god stood. Owned by Yen and Esther Tow, Diamond Head (named for Hawaii's famous dormant volcano) was a somewhat more modest venue leaning much further into the Hawaiian aesthetic than its larger cousin up the road. With its Waikiki Lounge and Royal Hawaiian bar, Diamond Head proffered "Hawaiian, American and Chinese Food at Its Best." Wicker egg chairs and more traditional seating surrounded the parquet floor; a piano was on hand to put guests in the mood for dancing. The by-now standard Polynesian pop décor was everywhere, from dangling fish floats to bamboo walls and native tiki masks.

Despite the sign outside proclaiming it as a Hawaiian restaurant, Diamond Head, like so many New England tiki destinations, was Chinese American first. Not that you'd know from the blurb heading the drink menu, which really doubled down on the Hawaiian theme: "From the blue Hawaiian shore of Waikiki, we bring you these delightful Hawaiian drinks to whet your appetite before your sumptuous dining." The "Hawaiian drinks" on offer were mostly Californian American—you've got your Scorpion Bowl, your Mai Tai, and, interestingly, something called a Tickle Dog—and the sumptuous dining likely referred to the inexpensive Chinese buffet.

If all that Chinese food and tiki grog didn't convince you that Diamond Head was foremost a Hawaiian establishment, the souvenirs would: matchbooks printed with Hawaiian scenes of outriggers sailing on a tumultuous sea beneath a tall mountain (volcano?), behind which peeked a setting orange sun. Their oval ceramic plates were impressive, printed with a more peaceful scene of a blue palm tree, islands dotting the ocean behind, and a lone outrigger sailing lonesome across the sea.

Unlike Kowloon, Diamond Head only managed to hang on for thirty years, closing in 1998, just long enough to become a lamented institution. Just off Route 1 in Lynnfield, the similarly venerated Bali Hai, opened and operated by James and Lillie Yee, managed to last a decade longer. Overlooking Suntaug Lake, Bali Hai had a few things in common with Diamond Head, starting with its modest exterior. Jutting up from the ground through the front of an otherwise level roof, Bali Hai's A-frame featured a sign lit from within. Its tiki idol, printed onto the sign rather than carved, was less Hawaiian than either Diamond Head's or Kowloon's, more impressionistic with spiral eyes, fangs, and two simple arrows crossing below. The name BALI HAI underscored this strange

Diamond Head matchbook. *Scott Schell.*

tiki, beckoning you to enter the door beneath the sign to find what treasures lay in wait.

Inside: tribal drums dangled from the ceiling above low Chinese dragons guarding the entryway of bamboo and the souvenir case; in later days, Keno screens would constantly glow from this area, clashing with the scenery. Bali Hai's ceramicware was impressive; like Diamond Head, it offered a take-away plate, this one round with an ombre sunburst pattern around the edge. A mountainous island in the upper left corner—the eponymous Bali Hai?—dwarfed the outriggers paddling toward it. The dinner menu (introduced in 1973) was far more illustrative than most tiki restaurants, this one depicting a scene of islanders at a feast. That theme carried through into the dining room, where hukilau scenes played out across backlit murals. Red vinyl booths sat under large tiki lights, no two the same; likely from Oceanic Arts, these lamps were constructed of bamboo and seashells, cane and rattan, all glowing serenely from within. If nothing else, Bali Hai was a fantastic place for indirect lighting.

Bali Hai postcard. *Scott Schell.*

When a fire broke out in the early 1970s, Bali Hai barely blinked. Unlike with the Bridgeport Hu Ke Lau or the Keentiki, Bali Hai weathered its inferno and kept tiki-ing on. The restaurant's downfall was nothing more dramatic than a sound wall, constructed along Route 128 in the early 2010s and blocking the distinct building from highway traffic. Though Bali Hai remained open until 2018 (still operated by the original owners!), the sound wall essentially doomed the business from its inception, making this tropical hideaway a little too hidden away.

Still, what's surprising isn't that Bali Hai closed in 2018 but that they made it that long. On the West Coast, tiki was falling out of fashion rapidly as the generation gap was yawning open. Tiki and faux Polynesia, which had partly been the Greatest Generation's way to escape the horrors of war and the mundanity of modern life by injecting some exoticism into their world, was now seen as square. Witco, the furniture and art company whose popularity surged during the first tiki boom, closed shop. The fleeting jungle fantasy of Witco couldn't compete with images from the real jungles of Vietnam on our 1970s TVs every night, and the tiki-restaurant charm of eating Asian food in ersatz huts covered in thatch felt increasingly inappropriate to the more radical Baby Boomer generation. Tiki was on its way out; in the words of Sven Kirsten, author of *The Book of Tiki*, the devolution had begun.

It just took New England a little longer to get the news.

Chapter 5

PINEAPPLE JUICE IN YOUR MAI TAI

TIKI DEVOLUTION COMES HOME

B oston metro's semi-operational subway and trolley system is known as the T, and the Red Line terminates at a station called Alewife (named, aptly, for a type of fish) in Cambridge. Near the station, Jasper White's Summer Shack casts an imposing figure. A popular seafood and corn dog joint, it's spawned locations in Boston and in the Mohegan Sun casino in Connecticut. But only the free-standing Cambridge establishment has a bizarrely proportioned statue out in front of its brick edifice, a long-faced fisherman with rain gear and a corncob pipe, the face looking like an absurdly stretched version of the Gorton's Fisherman mascot on all those packages of fish sticks. Near Gorton's of Gloucester (credited with inventing those fish sticks), a more proportional statue of a fisherman stands; erected in 1925, the legend on that statue reads, THEY THAT GO DOWN IN SHIPS 1623–1923.

A seafaring region, New England has long been a place with its own histories of coastal life and living with the ocean. Tiki fever might have come to New England, gripping it with a similar fervor to that of the rest of the country, but that fisherman with the elongated face and nose with the two coal-black eyes out in front of Summer Shack underscores a fundamental truth about New England: tiki was a borrowed history, and our homegrown legacies are stronger. That fisherman statue started out life as a carved moai, one of two flanking the entrance to the building eventually known as Summer Shack. But for a time, it was the Aku-Aku—named for Thor Heyerdahl's sequel to *Kon-Tiki*—and it already had deep roots in New England tiki.

Aku-Aku Worcester.
Scott Schell.

Skipper Kent and his wife, Lucille, had helped to kickstart the Northeast's sometimes intermittent fascination with tiki and Polynesian pop. As we've discussed, their Polynesian Village restaurant in the Somerset Hotel was a marvel of nautical and tiki immersion, operating in its original location until 1968. In came Bobby Seto, who managed the popular Ho Sai Gai restaurant in Boston's Chinatown, which was founded by his father, George. The younger Seto bought the Polynesian Village and moved it to its standalone location in Cambridge, rechristening it the Aku-Aku. Initially, this new location held fast to the tenets of the Polynesian Village—an overgrown tropical jungle look prevailed, with indoor palm trees and a large tiki at the entrance stand. Bamboo chairs welcomed visitors into this new/old tropical paradise, and shell lights and tapa-covered lanterns hung from the ceiling. It was, in short, the sort of tiki temple any self-respecting tikiphile would love to call their home bar, their tropical getaway close to home.

Other Massachusetts locations soon opened: one in Worcester and one in Boston, on Commonwealth Ave. A massive ship's wheel dominated the Lanuki Lounge in this latter destination, only to be outdone by the lighted aquarium tube (eight inches round, fifty feet long, claimed a postcard) circumnavigating the bar, filled with tropical fish. You could clip a coupon in your local newspaper to get "Free Hot Tea for Life" in a custom Aku-Aku thermos, and you could use the thermos at any Aku-Aku (or Ho Sai Gai) location. (The offer was only valid until Christmas Day 1977, so your chances of getting an Aku-Aku thermos now with that coupon are markedly slimmer.)

Even before its transformation into a brick building with its bizarre fisherman out front, the times would eventually change for the Cambridge

Aku-Aku thermos ad. *Author's collection.*

Aku-Aku. Inside, the rattan furniture would be replaced by neon Naugahyde, and the walls would be lined in velvet. There was still bamboo, still thatch, still tikis, but as the '70s marched on and became the '80s, tiki fever increasingly seemed to be happening in the rearview. Sven Kirsten's tiki devolution was starting to slink into the Atlantic Northeast.

Part of the devolution can be found in something as mundane as a supply company. When the first tiki restaurants and bars were being built, they were created by architects and designers with vision. Skilled carvers were called in, authentic artifacts were sourced (and authentic-ish artifacts were crafted), and whimsical elements like water features, bridges, and huts enclosing booths were the standard of the day. We've talked about Oceanic Arts, the tiki and tropical supply company in Whittier, California. As the grander visions of tiki began to fade, restaurateurs turned more and more to a paler, more economical supplier, one far more interested in mass production and ready-made bar décor than the far more personalized and thoughtful OA. It had a machine that once made plastic leis twenty-four hours a day. It shipped paper parasols in bulk from Korea. Its wall hangings were fiberglass, and its hula skirts were polyethylene and came in a variety of bright colors. Tiki in America has never been truly authentic—that's one of its appeals— but this stuff was like a copy of a copy of a copy, the fast fashion of ersatz tropical. This was Orchids of Hawaii.

Started by Tachio Uchida and Kei Yamato in 1952, Orchids of Hawaii was later passed down to Uchida's daughter Kim Mumola and her husband, Nicky. From its showroom and warehouse in the Bronx, New York, Orchids of Hawaii supplied Chinese- and Polynesian-style restaurants up and down the East Coast. Known now primarily for its steady supply of mass-produced and largely non-exclusive mugs—your basic Zombie, Fu Manchu, skull, panda—Orchids of Hawaii provided an easy template for restaurants and bars without the budget or desire for the more bespoke and elaborate Oceanic Arts. They also sold "bar mixes to make real Polynesian cocktails," such as orgeat and passion fruit syrup in gallon jugs, powdered lemon flavor— sweetened or unsweetened—or the worryingly vague Polynesian Cocktail Mix: "Perfect for any drink that requires fruit juice." Their catalogue came with a bartender's guide packed with recipes straight out of the ongoing devolution; the Mai Tai isn't made with pineapple juice, but it does curiously ask for orange juice—not to mention sweetened lime juice, preferably made from the Orchids powder mix. There was even an enticement to contact "'Kai'…the nation's foremost expect in Chinese and Polynesian restaurants." Kai was going to help you save money and make your restaurant look fantastic, and though he wouldn't help you build out your establishment himself, he would put you in contact with someone who could. Unfortunately, there's no indication that Kai was actually a real person, and the claim that he was a "foremost expert" in tiki environments was dubious at best.

Interest in tropical and tiki décor went through surges and droughts as the tiki devolution swept the country. In a 1989 article in the *New Yorker*, Nicky lamented, "Tropical went out when *Star Wars* came in.…Nobody wanted tropical. They wanted chrome and glass and gray rooms." While the article went on to say that tiki was making a minor comeback, Orchids of Hawaii didn't last much longer, closing up shop only five years later in 1994. One wonders what the Mumolas would have thought of the eventual merging of *Star Wars* and tiki into its own mini genre.

The legacy of Orchids of Hawaii is interesting nowadays. While much of their catalogue was made with inexpensive materials and would be considered cheap, Orchids' lamps were and still are considered somewhat high quality. And the mugs! Because they were mass-produced, a lot of those mugs are still around, with eBay selling scores of "vintage" 1970s mugs. What's more, Dynasty Wholesale, a restaurant supply company in Queens, New York, acquired some of the classic Orchids molds. Nowadays, most tiki bars—even the really good ones—will have a few of these classic designs on their shelves. The old adage is true: you stick around long enough, you eventually gain respectability. Today's trash can become tomorrow's treasure, and as we've seen with everything from breakfast cereal to toys to lunchboxes, it sometimes helps if it was mass produced in the latter decades of the twentieth century.

Back to the devolution: in other parts of the country, it seemed to happen more rapidly and earlier. Maybe that's because places like Southern California embraced the initial waves of Polynesian pop so thoroughly and so ubiquitously that the tatters of the trend were that much more obvious. Apartment buildings and bowling alleys with tiki themes began to look dated, and tiki bars and restaurants faded away. More insidiously, some of these bars realized they didn't need to use the top-shelf alcohol and fresh ingredients that had always defined the work of Donn Beach, Vic Bergeron, and their contemporaries.

It would be easy to lay the fall of an entire cocktail movement at the foot of a single drink—easy and probably wrong. But it's interesting to consider the fate of the Mai Tai, invented by Trader Vic Bergeron in 1944 and one of tiki's most famous cocktails (only Donn Beach's Zombie has a similar cachet, and even that hasn't approached the Mai Tai's mainstream ubiquity). According to tiki mixologist and historian Jeff "Beachbum" Berry, Vic's concoction was constructed as follows:

1 ounce fresh lime juice
½ ounce orange curaçao
¼ ounce orgeat syrup
¼ ounce sugar syrup
1 ounce dark Jamaican rum
1 ounce aged Martinique rum

Shake well with plenty of crushed ice. Serve in a double old-fashioned glass. Sink your spent lime shell into the drink. Garnish with a mint sprig.

The cocktail follows the classic Barbadian rhyme, "One of sour, two of sweet, three of strong, four of weak." Fresh lime for the sour, the sugar syrup and orgeat for the sweet, the rums and curaçao for the strong, and then "plenty of ice" for dilution. Balanced and delicious, Vic first served the libation to visiting Tahitian friends, who exclaimed *Maita'i roa a'e*! which translates to "out of this world! The best!" The Mai Tai was born.

There have been riffs on the original Mai Tai since the beginning. The Don the Beachcomber "swizzle" version—adding grapefruit juice, swapping out orgeat for falernum and Martinique rum for Cuban, and dropping in some Pernod—arrived in the 1950s. Some claim that Vic's Mai Tai is really just a version of Donn's Q.B. Cooler, but in his book, *Trader Vic's Bartender's Guide*, Vic refutes this claim quite vehemently: "Anyone who says I didn't create this drink is a dirty stinker."

In 1971, the Surf Bar at the Royal Hawaiian Hotel in Waikiki became the first place to add pineapple juice to its Mai Tai, not to mention orange and lemon juice, with a sugar cane stick dipped into the glass for garnish. This seems to be the version that bars would later utilize as their template, using it to build even more fruity and sugary drinks. A recent Mai Tai recipe from the site Allrecipes.com recommends this construction:

1 cup ice cubes
3 fluid ounces pineapple juice
2 fluid ounces orange juice
1 (1.5-fluid-ounce) jigger spiced rum
½ (1.5-fluid-ounce) jigger coconut-flavored rum
1 teaspoon grenadine syrup

Shake and serve.

Nothing sour, and the fruit juice and the grenadine overpower the rum (whose provenance is no longer important) so much that it becomes nearly impossible to taste it. That may be part of this version's appeal. If you can't really taste the alcohol, it becomes even easier to pound them back when you're on vacation. Remember my first bout with a Scorpion Bowl? Bars save money when they don't have to purchase sourced rums and they don't even need to make or buy orgeat or falernum. A would-be mixologist can easily re-create this version at home.

It's not really a Mai Tai, though, and as goes the Mai Tai, so goes the world. Tiki drinks became known as "fruity umbrella drinks" with no real place in the world of serious cocktails. It was these drinks that were and are generally served in New England's Chinese restaurants with tiki-lite overlays. If we can't blame the existence of these establishments for the devolution of tiki (their concurrent rise with "authentic" tiki places means we can't really dismiss them as a subsequent link in a broken chain), we can maybe point to these cocktails as a contributing factor. It would be a long while before tiki drinks reclaimed their origins and started, maybe for the first time, to garner some respect. What America wanted as tiki fever faded was cheap rum and cheaper canned fruit juice to give everything a vaguely fruity, vaguely tropical feel. And even if that's not what America wanted, that's what America got—even, eventually, in New England.

But there's a curious history in the region, one we've touched on from time to time in this book but haven't really explored. The rise of what one would call the "authentic" tiki/Polynesian pop restaurant and bar was, in New England, concurrent with the idea of the basic Chinese American restaurant with some light Polynesian theming and tropical drinks. In other parts of the country, that ersatz riff on an ersatz riff spelled absolute doom of the "authentically inauthentic" vibe of what American tiki was supposed to be about. But in New England, tiki had been riffing on itself since almost the start. Despite some impossible-to-deny tiki temples in the region (Kowloon, a Hu Ke Lau here and there), those Chinese restaurants with their light dusting of South Seas flair were a defining characteristic of the region. While I wouldn't go so far as to say these places are what we should think about when we think of tiki, I believe dismissing them outright as a product of devolution is also a mistake.

Defining tiki is always going to be somewhat of a subjective exercise. What makes a tiki place a tiki place? Is it the décor? The tiny Tiki Island in Medford, Massachusetts, serves Chinese American food and standard cocktails, but there's a great island-themed mural inside and a moai in the lobby. The Ho Kong in Woonsocket, Rhode Island, is full of tiki theming mixed with Chinese imagery—dragons wrapped around pillars in front of a check-in desk with tiki masks on the wall behind. Is it the presence of actual tikis? The Grand China in Salem, New Hampshire, was a Bavarian-style building whose white outer surfaces were intermittently painted with Polynesian patterns and oddly shaped tiki masks; its shortened A-frame did nothing to enhance the idea of this as a tiki destination. (Nor did a 2013 admonition on restaurant review site FourSquare: "Try not to touch anything, it's probably sticky.") What about heritage and longevity? The Hawaiian Isle in Plaistow, New Hampshire, opened in the early 1970s, and despite the presence of some tikis and tapa lanterns, it remains foremost a Chinese restaurant with wall-to-wall Chinese décor. Yet it's thought of fondly by New England tiki aficionados, especially in light of its failed sequel, Concorde's Hawaiian Isle II. Despite a promising full-size A-frame out front, the interior of II was decidedly non-tiki and closed in 2006.

That's not to say that the tiki trend entirely stopped during this phase. The Kohala Mauna opened in 1970 in South Burlington, Vermont. Its name appeared in an amazing bamboo font in ads and on matchbooks, and early press promised a "Traditional Hawaiian Luau"—all this, despite the location looking more like a Cracker Barrel than a South Seas getaway on the outside. The Kohala Mauna's Island Lounge was joined in 1975 by a "new intimate lounge" following an expansion. Elsewhere in Vermont, the Beachcomber Lounge opened at the Bonnie Oaks Lodge and Bungalows in Fairlee, right on Lake Morley. Impressively laden with bamboo and thatch, this early 1970s lounge had tapa cloth–style wallpaper, fake palms growing from floor to ceiling, and decorative giant clamshells hanging from the walls. Menacing moai heads peered out over the lounge, just above the extremely New England stone fireplace, a retrofit culture clash below the hanging fishnets.

For many establishments, it wasn't *devolution* so much as *de-emphasis*. The mighty Kowloon in Saugus expanded its menu exponentially over

Beachcomber Lounge, Bonnie Oaks postcard. *Author's collection.*

the years, growing from a half-and-half Chinese and American menu to encompass Polynesian, Sichuan, Thai, and Japanese cuisines, including sushi. The restaurant itself grew as its kitchens became a pan-Asian culinary wonderland, opening a comedy club in the 1990s (Kowloon Komedy, where luminaries like Jerry Seinfeld, Phyllis Diller, and Dane Cook have performed) and the ultra-modern Hong Kong Lounge in 2011, complete with big-screen TVs. Tikis could and would still be found in this evolving environment, but now the wonderfully weird sensation of eating on a boat in the middle of a restaurant, a constantly erupting volcano to one side and a lagoon to the other, was distinctly a kitschy throwback. Those areas were fully ensconced in the past, separate from Kowloon's present and certainly removed from its future.

Tiki had always been about invented escapes, a concept of island life that was part idealized memory and part Hollywood magic. As the twentieth century waned and Americans moved further and further from the tiki heyday of the 1960s, it seemed that we would forever lose touch with the haunting, thrilling enchantment of classic Polynesian pop. Elsewhere, tiki had been celebrated on a grand scale with large budgets and expert architects; by contrast, many of New England's tiki escapes were more modest and disappeared more quietly and on a slower timeline. In New England, home of alewives and whaling and islands that got bracingly cold in the winter, we took what we wanted from tiki—just the basics—and discarded the rest. The days of full faux island immersion were long gone and were never coming back.

Except that something was happening in America that no one really anticipated. A convergence from the underground of disparate forces was slowly coming together, a radical collision of the worlds of punk rock music, the craft cocktail movement, and fancy coffee table books full of supposedly square nostalgia.

Even as New England inched away from tiki, tiki was clawing its way back from the dead. We just didn't know it yet.

Chapter 6

REVIVAL

*D*id tiki in America ever really go away? Certainly its hold on the mainstream—dominant on the West Coast, less so in New England— dwindled over the years; as generations changed, new bar concepts rushed in to take its place, and the term *tiki* became synonymous with fruity umbrella drinks lacking class, taste, or refinement.

"In the 80s," said Sven Kirsten, author of *The Book of Tiki*, "many Tiki temples closed or got renovated into more generic places. This devolution included throwing out the beachcomber lamps as 'dust catchers,' painting the Tikis in bright colors, getting rid of maintenance-heavy water features, and cutting off wood rot–weakened outrigger beams." He also credits some of the devolution to owner burnout; it's hard to invent a slice of paradise and then make it consistently profitable. "The cuisine stayed the same, the drinks had a high profit margin, and the standard décor was supplied by Orchids of Hawaii or Witco—especially on the east coast, far away from Oceanic Arts and other suppliers."

"Orchids of Hawaii was very strong and influential on the East Coast," agreed Otto Von Stroheim, whom we'll meet in a moment, "and provided a cookie cutter package for restaurants, so any Chinese restaurant could look pretty good overnight for a few thousand dollars."

Still, there were places in which the dream of tiki lived on. Backyard luaus had their heyday in the 1960s, but they didn't really stop. Ditto home tiki bars; even as aboveground Polynesian pop escapes dwindled, folks began hanging up thatch and bamboo in basements and rec rooms and serving Mai Tais to their friends.

Kahiki Moon dining area. *James Kathary.*

In the 1990s, America's dominant culture was shifting away from Baby Boomers and toward the more cynical and disaffected Generation X. Dubbed "slackers," this new generation was raised as latchkey kids and was typified in the media as being wary of earnestness and reluctant to embrace adulthood. On one hand, they came of age in an era of economic prosperity and the optimism of the early internet; on the other, they were forced to reckon with and to effect massive social change, dealing with things like the AIDS crisis, racism and homophobia, and the crack epidemic.

And tiki, of all things, started surfacing above the morass.

Otto Von Stroheim, a Southern California graphic designer and punk music fan, was compelled by the Midcentury tiki aesthetic. He collected old tiki mugs from often-defunct tiki establishments and visited Los Angeles–based tropical bars to take in shows from neo-lounge acts like Combustible Edison. The décor was good and the music was great, but the drinks were a far cry from what they had been in the heyday. Von Stroheim told *Punch* magazine, "You'd order a Manhattan or a Martini and the bartender would say, 'Oh wow, a Martini! Let me look up how to make that.'" He should have visited Brother Cleve at the Rathskeller.

If cocktail crafting had strayed far from Donn Beach's Rhum Rhapsodies, music was growing more interesting. As a way for Gen X to contextualize their emotions and thoughts about the disparate forces at work in society, mainstream pop embraced new sounds and concepts: grunge grew dominant very quickly, and rap and hip-hop moved to the forefront of musical expression. As counterculture became culture, previously underground music scenes had to reconsider where to go. Punk, which had defined the counterculture in prior decades, was edging out of its relevance. "Between 1980 and 1984, punks were moving beyond punk and were disillusioned with what the subsequent generation of punks were offering," Von Stroheim explained. "Punks turned to other music genres like New Country, industrial music, and lost lounge music like Esquivel and The Three Suns. Exotica was a known subgenre of jazz and lounge, and Martin Denny became a prominent figure in the new Lounge movement right up there with Esquivel." This new aesthetic hit the mainstream when Capitol Records began releasing its Ultra-Lounge series in 1996, beginning with the compilation *Mondo Exotica*, featuring the likes of Les Baxter, Yma Sumac, and, of course, Martin Denny.

In 1995, Otto Von Stroheim produced the first issue of *Tiki News*, a zine about tiki whose primary focus was mug trading. "I figured, hey, I got fifty or sixty mugs, there's gotta be somebody in, like, Phoenix with fifty or sixty mugs from the bars around them that wants mine from, say, the Outrigger in Monterey." No one had ever published a magazine about tiki before, and it attracted the likes of the prime movers of the tiki revival: folks like Sven Kirsten, tiki historian; Jeff "Beachbum" Berry, then a part-time amateur mixologist; Josh "SHAG" Agle, illustrator and artist; Bosko Hrnjak, renowned tiki carver; and Baby Doe, creator of the internet's first tiki-based website, *Baby Doe's Obsessed*. All these people in *Tiki News*'s orbit would grow to define what tiki would come to mean in this new era, as *Tiki News* itself became a sensation, eventually gaining distribution in record stores worldwide.

But it was still early days for the revival. Folks were interested in tiki, but the movement was still underground. Other portents were on the horizon, though. In 1987, New York's legendary Rainbow Room reopened in Rockefeller Center; owner Dale DeGroff simultaneously sought to celebrate the bar's Prohibition-era beginnings while also elevating its wares. Classic recipes reinterpreted with fresh ingredients and top-shelf alcohol were joined by new cocktails made in the same vein. Nearby bar The Odeon introduced the Cosmopolitan—a vodka martini with cranberry juice, lime juice, and triple sec—and Sasha Petraske's Milk & Honey promoted the pleasures of a quiet, grown-up bar where high-quality cocktails were matched only by high-quality clientele. As the era of the speakeasy became the focal point of this early craft cocktail movement, so did the theater of the speakeasy: some bars were hidden behind bookcases or accessed through phone booths. Sure, it was gimmicky, but it underscored a sense of mystery and thrill that had gotten lost in the '70s pickup-bar scene and the wild excesses (and diminishing authenticity) of the 1980s.

And what of tiki drinks? If they were thought of at all, they were considered part of the problem. They were thought of as those fruity umbrella drinks, slushy and processed, made of the worst ingredients. The kind of drink made for people who liked to pretend they weren't drinking. Enter Jeff Berry, a filmmaking student from California, who discovered that some Los Angeles–based bars were still making cocktails the old-fashioned way, with fresh citrus, high-quality liquor, and crafted mixers. In fact, places like the Tiki-Ti in Los Angeles and the still-hanging-on Trader Vic's in Beverly Hills were making, in his words, the "only 'craft' cocktails to be had in the 1980s." In a world where artificial drink mixes were the standard of the day, these very few locations still cared about what went into a good cocktail.

Berry's decision to get serious about cocktails was met with some resistance. While Trader Vic had published a bartending guide in 1947 (with intermittent revisions over the years), most classic tiki recipes were hard to source. Donn Beach had learned his lesson from Monte Proser and the purloined Zombie and had kept his recipes not only under lock and key but also as true mysteries. Even if you could find his old notes or those of his bartenders, some ingredients were impossible to decode. What were "Don's Spices #2"? What was a "gardenia mix"? And what the heck was "munrelaf"? (This last was the mixer "falernum"—spelled backward.)

It was a painstaking process to unlock a lot of these old recipes. Berry talked with Donn's old bartenders if he could find them, and in a coup, Donn's family sent him a photocopied bartending guide from the man himself (riddled with his inexplicable ciphers, of course). His wife, Annene, a former bartender, helped him to reverse-engineer some of these old recipes. And he began experimenting on his own. Eventually, cohesive drinks made with real ingredients began to coalesce, and he shared them with his friends in the nascent tiki revival movement—not that anyone really knew there was a movement then. Not just yet.

Small indicators of a resurgence were cropping up, mostly around Southern California. Disney, which had given the initial movement a cultural toehold with Disneyland's Enchanted Tiki Room and its Tahitian Terrace—

complete with luau and (nonalcoholic) tropical drinks. Now, it had produced two artists named Kevin Kidney and Jody Daley who would help define tiki for a new age. Their 1996 presentation at the Anaheim Museum, *Tiki: Native Drums in the Orange Grove*, explored the art, architecture, and cultural impact of the original scene, arguing for its relevance. Through its exhibits, exhaustive cultural spelunking, and even its gift shop, *Native Drums in the Orange Grove* provided a key for nascent tikiphiles. Said Sven Kirsten, "We cannot predict the future influence of the Anaheim Museum show, but it will undoubtedly have left it's [*sic*] impression on some sleeping genius."

One of those sleeping geniuses was Kirsten himself. Perhaps the most important inflection point of the tiki revival came when Sven Kirsten published his *Book of Tiki* in 2000. It was a massive Taschen tome that functioned as a primer for all things tiki, starting by going back to the South Pacific and laying out the actual history of the Tiki idol as a representation of the world's first man. From there, Kirsten's book touched on everything from the early bartenders to the tiki architecture boom, *Kon-Tiki* and *Tales of the South Pacific*, exotica music, and black velvet art. It even included a chapter by Jeff "Beachbum" Berry on classic tiki cocktails. It was the first book that looked at tiki as a legitimate art form and a major cultural force, inventing the term "Polynesian pop" and celebrating the Midcentury craze as something worthy of critical notice. It was *Native Drums in the Orange Grove* writ large and in book form, expanding the scope of tiki beyond Southern California (though, it must be noted, rarely into the realm of New England).

The influence of *The Book of Tiki*, not only on the revival but also on the definition of the genre *as* a genre, cannot be overstated. Kirsten said:

> *Even in its heyday in the midcentury, the phenomenon was not recognized as a cohesive style*—The Book of Tiki *did that for the first time, and it gave it its name, "Tiki." Nowadays, no one can remember what an absolute vacuum, a black hole existed where now* [there] *are thousands of hits for the term. The name Don the Beachcomber: forgotten. Witco: never heard of before. Apartments, motels, Tiki amusement parks…unheard of.*

Now armed with a definition and a cultural jumping-off point, tiki could begin a revival in earnest. Important new bars began popping up all over California, like Forbidden Island in Alameda, opened by brothers Michael and Emmanuel Thanos and Martin Cate, the latter of whom would eventually strike out on his own with a new bar in San Francisco called Smuggler's Cove. This bar became another focal point for tiki legitimacy when Cate won a prestigious James Beard Award for his book of recipes and tiki history, also titled *Smuggler's Cove*. In New Orleans, Beachbum Berry opened Latitude 29 (proving that tiki bars beyond California could still be successful) and began releasing books filled with those unearthed and reverse-engineered drinks. His *Grog Log*, *Sippin' Safari*, and *Potions of the Caribbean* would all prove important, influential guides through the world of exotic cocktails— not just the recipes but also the history and cultural context behind those recipes. Even Witco, the tropical art and furniture supply company, staged something of a comeback: William Westenhaver had never stopped carving and eventually taught all he knew to his grandson-in-law, Ken Pleasant. Ken and his wife, Heather, retained the Witco trademark and all the copyrighted designs and began their own company, Pleasant Tiki; their Witco Décor by Pleasant Tiki re-creates classic carvings as well as new work.

All at once, people were looking beyond the kitsch and the camp of tiki and finding something worthy there—and maybe the kitsch and the camp are part of *why* it's worthy. As with so many previous elements of so-called disposable pop culture, from toys to comics to 1980s horror novels and beyond, a new generation was discovering the inherent value in these things once deemed silly or trashy.

The music, the books, the bars, the cocktails, the architecture—tiki was returning in an entirely new world, one far more connected and interactive. Websites like Tiki Central brought a sense of community and forward momentum to people who had previously thought they were alone in their love of tiki. Big events like California's Tiki Oasis and Florida's Hukilau brought together scores of people in aloha shirts and muumuus, with people teaching symposiums on tiki history, offering bespoke rum tastings, and having the sort of backyard luau writ large never dreamed of in the days of tiki's first cultural flashpoint.

And among all this, what of New England?

It was started, of all places, in Vermont, by a Northern California DJ named James Kathary.

Growing up in the Bay Area during the height of the area's tiki and South Seas fascination had easily stoked young Kathary's obsession with Hawai'i and Hawaiiana. His Auntie Diane also fueled the fire: in the '60s, she would visit the islands in the summer and return, loaded with tales and souvenirs. As the '60s moved into the '70s and '80s, young Kathary and his mom would spend weeks with Diane on the islands experiencing the culture, the sounds of Don Ho and others, and "even chasing Jack Lord (*Hawaii 5-0*) and Tom Selleck (*Magnum P.I.*) around the islands." By the early 1990s, Kathary was

Kahiki Moon entrance. *James Kathary.*

eager to escape the California rave scene for "some fresh air" and hopped in a cab bound for Burlington, Vermont. It was a good move—he met his wife, Bridget, there—but soon enough he grew to miss all the Hawaiian influences that had defined his childhood and early adulthood.

"In the late '90s, Hawai'i was popping up on the radar heavy…[and] it was time to bring it back," Kathary said in an interview. "I was just pumping Hawai'i out there, in graphic design and other things…and I had this beautiful basement place in a giant Victorian building, that I turned into an arcade/rave/tiki bar.…We played house music with a Hawai'i theme. It wasn't *tiki* per se, it was just hardcore Hawaiiana." By the early aughts, however, as Polynesian pop was getting its first real foothold in the country beyond California, Kathary turned his focus to tiki specifically. Following an impromptu trip to Chicago for the early tiki event Exotica 2003, he looked to his adopted backyard of Burlington, Vermont.

The "authentically inauthentic" ethos of tiki, which had only briefly kissed New England during the trend's most significant early years, was now almost impossible to find. A few leftovers remained: Kowloon still stood sentry in its place on Route 1 in Massachusetts, its massive Hawaiian Kū always keeping watch, and Chicopee's Hu Ke Lau was still hanging on. But while the multiple "Chinese American restaurants with slapdash tropical cocktails" trendlet had never gone away, the true tiki Renaissance that the West Coast was enjoying was thin on the ground. "There was nothing here, and I did it," Kathary laughed. This wasn't entirely true; while New Hampshire's King Tiki beat him by a couple years, it was gone by the time Kathary rose to meet the moment. He selected the basement of an office building in downtown Burlington, once occupied by a Mexican restaurant, and sought to convince investors that tiki was the next big thing.

To do that, Kathary resorted to drastic measures. "I took Sven Kirsten's *Book of Tiki* and cut it up." This was the logical endpoint for a book that existed to create a shorthand vernacular for anyone interested in the disparate diaspora of tiki. No longer just a reference guide, now Kirsten's book could double as a blueprint. Supplementing Kirsten's pictures were Kathary's hand-drawn concepts for how best to outfit the 3,500-square-foot space, which included a 1,000-square-foot kitchen. The investors bit, and soon James Kathary—adopting the moniker Primo Kimo—was crafting his subterranean paradise. Intentionally avoiding the word "tiki"—soon a common practice in the revivalist New England Poly-pop vernacular—Primo Kimo billed his new establishment as a Polynesian Restaurant and Lounge. And its name was Kahiki Moon.

Since the demise of Kohala Mauna, Vermont hadn't seen anything really like it—and maybe not even then. Kathary brought in the big (kahuna) guns when it came to décor: Oceanic Arts, Ken Pleasant (Witco Décor by Pleasant Tiki), Miles Thompson, Woody Greenwood, Scott Schiedly—all incomparable talents in the burgeoning new world of tiki. You started in the otherwise anodyne lobby of an office building, with an imposing door flanked by two carved tiki totems inviting you to open it and discover the realm beyond. A small wooden sign reading KAHIKI MOON affixed to the wall right of the door only added to the sense of mystery and excitement. The doorway led to a dark stairwell beckoning you underground, and it became immediately apparent that you were in an entirely new world. The brick walls faded into the background, overlain with bamboo-framed exotica records and paintings of tikis. The L-shaped bar, overhung with a thatch and bamboo roof, was coated in clear acrylic, through which patrons could see classic tiki bar postcards and paper ephemera from days gone by. Indirect lighting showcased the elaborate carvings, the fish floats, the fake palms, the swizzle stick collection, and the tiki masks hung on the wall. Every barstool was a hand-carved tiki statue, grimly but efficiently holding up the awestruck

Kahiki Moon lobby. *James Kathary.*

Kahiki Moon bar. *James Kathary.*

patrons, and every booth was an alcove of shadowy seclusion. A trio of pufferfish lamps hung behind the bar, illuminating the extensive collection of spirits; within two months of operation, Kahiki Moon was Vermont's largest buyer of rum. Be sure to sip the Kahiki Moonlight in Vermont, the bar's signature cocktail.

The food, often an afterthought in these tropical establishments, was top-notch; chef Steven Gross (previously of New York City's Zoë and The French Laundry in Napa) helped Kahiki Moon become known as a fine dining establishment lurking in the shadows of a Poly-pop dreamland. Duck breast, calamari, and goat cheese risotto with squash and spinach was among the many dishes that cemented Kahiki Moon's reputation not just as a knock-out atmospheric bar but as an actual foodie destination.

Kahiki Moon hit all the right markers: the food was fantastic, the drinks were on point, the décor was astounding. Exotica and lounge from Martin Denny on up suffused the atmosphere until ten o'clock, when the music kicked into high gear and a DJ would spin beach party jams to get people on their feet for a night of tropical dancing. Above all, the place was popular, bringing in the sort of money that usually keeps new restaurants afloat.

Kahiki Moon closed within nine months of operation.

As it turns out, creating paradise is easier than maintaining it. What James Kathary learned was what so many of the original tiki bar owners and restaurateurs learned: reality has a way of interfering with fantasy. In Kathary's case, it came down to operations. No matter how beautiful and well-appointed your location is, no matter how classic the décor or how diverse and expansive the rum selection is, none of it works without experience in running a restaurant and a bar. That lack of experience—not to mention staff who didn't entirely share his passion for what he was trying to accomplish—sank Kathary's dream. Following Kahiki Moon's demise, Primo Kimo attempted to craft a proposal for the upcoming Forbidden Island in Alameda, California, the first Polynesian pop establishment in which famed tiki expert and restaurateur Martin Cate had a hand in crafting. Though Kathary lost out on the bid, some of his Kahiki Moon artifacts ended up moving across the country to Alameda, meaning that, in a roundabout way, Primo Kimo's aesthetic finally ended up contributing to that faraway locale.

But Alameda's gain was New England's loss, and tiki was still having a heck of a time gaining traction in the northeastern United States. New Hampshire's attempt, King Tiki, disappeared almost as rapidly as Kahiki Moon. Owners Melissa and Robert Jasper were as into Hawaiiana as

James Kathary, outfitting their place in Midcentury island décor and tiki memorabilia. They were also coming from the type of experience Kathary didn't have, owning and operating the very successful retro breakfast franchise The Friendly Toast. Opening in 2000, the well-appointed King Tiki, which included two bars, a dining room, and a game room, was immediately beset by trouble on two sides. Unlike at Primo Kimo's place, the clientele of King Tiki didn't seem to understand what tiki was. Terence Gunn, a local DJ formerly of Seattle, who had occasion to work with King Tiki, explained the conundrum, as reported on the Tiki Central website:

> All the punters who frequent King Tiki are still stuck in the late 1980s; still into punk, new wave, heavy metal, and alternative (as well as, of course, rap and hip-hop). Lots of dopey college kids dressed in drab drinking Pabst Blue Ribbon out of a can. King Tiki's most successful night is Thursday night's Heavy Metal Karaoke. That should give an idea of what the place has turned into. It's really too bad. The place is absolutely fantastic, and the owners, Robert and Melissa Jasper, are genuinely into the whole retro scene and are two of the most generous, friendly people I've ever met. The biggest problem, however, is the rent they pay—a whopping $8000/ month. They've only been barely breaking even, and solely relying on their other business, The Friendly Toast, to carrying them through. It's a pity I didn't live here a couple years ago—or they, likewise, in Seattle. Things could've turned out much different for them.

That Portsmouth, New Hampshire's punk scene hadn't yet kindled to the retro-lounge movement illustrates how New England seemed to be behind the times when it came to these new tiki revivalist locations. Though the renaissance was in full swing in other parts of the country, maybe King Tiki and Kahiki Moon were just too early for the Northeast.

But there were other reasons why tiki was having such a problem latching onto New England's cultural landscape. There was a growing sensitivity to the concept of cultural appropriation and its ties to colonialism. The argument that Americans are exploiting the cultures of the South Pacific for pure entertainment holds some water: a major facet of early Polynesian pop in America was the concept of the civilized man in a place of savages. Films and stories of the era double down on the concept, both titillating with the idea of straight white men falling for the darker-skinned heathen women (and vice versa) and demonizing those cultures by inserting a white savior to help show them the error of their ways. It's an uncomfortable reality of the past, but it doesn't tell the entire story. Since the beginning, tiki in America has represented a merging of multiple cultures—not just the polycultures of the South Pacific but also elements from China, the Caribbean, and even parts of Africa. While the melding of these disparate influences can be read as an "othering," a way to treat any culture that isn't white, heterosexual, Christian, and American as exotic and primitive, it also becomes a brand-new expression unto itself, one so removed from its antecedents that it can be understood as something unique. Moreover, newer generations, armed with a cultural curiosity and sensitivity their forebears might not have possessed, dive into tiki more aware of—and more thoughtful about—the sort of representations they employ.

In New England, authenticity is almost bizarrely easy to come by, and for those intrigued by the American interpretation of tiki, all it costs is the price of a museum ticket to see the real thing. The Peabody Essex Museum in Salem, Massachusetts, has an impressive Oceanic art section going all the way back to the beginning of this book: whalers, traders, and other sea captains traveled from ports in New England to the wide world, including Polynesia and the South Pacific, bringing back artifacts and treasures. One optimistically hopes that these items were all legitimately traded and bartered for and not acquired through nefarious means. An article from the *Rapa Nui Journal* expands on this, highlighting one of the museum's most prized collections:

> *The Peabody Essex Museum in Salem, Massachusetts is in the possession of one of the finest collections of Rapanui wood carving in the world. This collection greatly benefited from New England being the hub of the world's whaling industry at the beginning of the 19th century. American whaleships started cruising the southeastern Pacific off the coast of South America from 1789 onwards. At the same time, several European countries were also sending their whaleships, but those were also captained and crewed mostly by Americans....Hawai'i also emerged as a hub for those whalers and fur traders operating in the Pacific. The first whaleship had already visited Easter Island in 1797....Whalers often bartered with the native inhabitants of various Pacific islands. Although food and water were the main bartered commodities, objects of art were also frequently traded. Those brought back by the sailors were passed on to their families and often eventually ended up in one of New England's museums. The bulk of the objects known today are held in the Peabody Museums in Cambridge and Salem.*

The article goes on to explain the unusual diversity of the artifacts, including two *moko* figurines not known to exist in any public or private collection in the world. And then there's the Kū, highlighted on the museum's website:

> *One of only three temple images of its kind in the world, the ancient Hawaiian god Kū occupies a place of honor in PEM's dramatic 2019 wing. A master carver created this* ki'i *of Kū, more famously known in his warring form of Kūkā'ilimoku ("snatcher of land"), for a* heiau *(temple) of the great chief and warrior Kamehameha I, who united the Hawaiian Islands in the early nineteenth century. At PEM, Kū can be understood as a manifestation of mana and a visual representation of Native Hawaiian agency. The Oceanic collection remains vital as we honor the many objects that embody spiritual, functional, and celebratory traditions, linking past generations to the present and future.*

In other words, you can travel to Saugus to see the carved Oceanic Arts' Kū standing high above Kowloon's entrance, and then you can head out to Salem to see the Kū carved by Oceanic artists.

If you want real Polynesia, New England can offer real Polynesia. However, in the ninety years since Donn Beach opened his first bar, the tiki trend has progressed so far away from actual Polynesian culture that the tiki we think of today is far removed from the origins of Tiki (with a capital T). Midcentury Americans appropriated (and, to be fair, celebrated) cultures they didn't entirely understand through the filters of Hollywood and hazy memories. From there, we made riffs on the original concepts, fantasias on fantasies, evolution and devolution and reinvention. It may be safe to say that the tiki of today is almost entirely invented rather than purloined or appropriated. Even still, many bars and restaurants have moved away from the trappings of what tiki and faux-Polynesia means, focusing instead on the broader concepts of tropical escapism, nautical elements like fish floats and netting, and some touches of Midcentury American kitsch like black velvet paintings. Cocktails take center stage, and if there's exotica on the playlist and tiki mugs on the shelves (many of which don't depict actual tikis), those seem to be somewhat acceptable holdovers from a bygone era.

Which is all to the good, but here we have a second issue, where we are trying to define what tiki is for a modern age. Does it lie in the past? Remember: neither Donn Beach nor Trader Vic brought tiki into the American parlance. Stephen Crane, the somewhat forgotten third progenitor of the tropical bar movement, introduced tikis as a design element and as an overarching

Hawaiian Kū at Peabody Essex Museum. *Gabriel Bascom.*

aesthetic, giving the movement its name and an iconography around which to coalesce. Eventually, Don the Beachcomber's and Trader Vic's added tikis to their establishments, but it's somewhat ironic that the Godfather of Tiki, Donn Beach, didn't invent the tiki bar. So what of new tropical/nautical/island-themed bars that de-emphasize tiki or that don't include tikis as a design element? Are those tiki bars? For many, the answer is no, even though we retroactively accept those proto-tiki bars as crucial and unreservedly "tiki." These juxtapositions are everywhere: we can note the disparaging term "Disney tiki," meaning tikis painted in the style of Disneyland's Enchanted Tiki Room, even though the Tiki Room was a definite steppingstone in the original Polynesian pop trend and has served as a gateway for generations of tiki enthusiasts. Instagram accounts like ThisAintTiki gatekeep the idea of what tiki is and should be, even though some of the arguments for and against seem somewhat arbitrary. (For example: is *Star Wars* tiki a legitimate offshoot of mainstream tiki? And does it even matter?)

On one hand, we have a vocal contingent with strict guidelines as to what tiki is and should be, and on the other, we have an equally vocal contingent that decries everything about tiki as cultural appropriation and colonialism. This latter point is further complicated by the "morbid and somewhat flagellant fascination on the part of late nineteenth century New Englanders with the sins of their forefathers." Historian George McCusker could well have been writing about New Englanders in the twenty-first century, so desperate to feel bad about the missteps and misdeeds of previous generations that we sometimes find it difficult to reckon with the fact that we have made real progress in taking accountability for our transgressions, in understanding and listening to the people whose cultures tiki came from, and reconciling that with our ongoing interest in American tropical escapism.

It is into this environment that modern tiki bars must try to forge ahead, and some brave souls did just that, each going about it in their own way. Portland, Maine's Rhum Food & Grog delved deep into the history and mystery of tiki, paying homage to those lounges of old while conjuring up something new. The mission statement on their website was alluring:

> *Escape the everyday and step into the subterranean hideout that is Rhum. Enjoy our well-crafted classic and contemporary cocktails, elevated Tiki fare, and uncommon raw bar, all in a lush atmosphere that brings the tropical South Seas to the frigid Northeast's doorstep.*
>
> *Rhum is a tribute to the classic Tiki bars of yesterday, as well as to the craft and romance of rum and its long tradition.*

The massive bar, overhung with a thatch roof, bisected the room, while clusters of multicolored fish floats demarcated cove-ish lounge areas. In this subterranean getaway, that delicious tiki-bar gloom pervaded, and though there were big-screen TVs, they tended to play surf movies and underwater scenes. Rhum's nautical bent extended to its octopus mascot, whose tentacles served as the bathroom door handles. Tikis hung on the walls, and the classic drink menu with its (Trader Vic original) Mai Tai, its Painkiller, and its Singapore Sling solidified the old-school tiki vibe that a place like Kahiki Moon captured so well. Even their original cocktail menu featured an updated riff on the Zombie—called the Dead on Arrival—and signified only two per customer in the classic Donn Beach tradition.

But again, quality and popularity did not spell long-term success, and Rhum closed its doors after about a year in business. I'll say it again: one of the most frustrating things about tiki temples is that, even when they're at their peak of quality and popularity, their fate always seems precarious. Tiki is a hard business, ironically for something so invested in a chill sensibility. Sometimes, even though the intention is right, tiki just doesn't work in the space it's occupying; see Boston's Tiki Rock, for example. Initially, Tiki Rock was supposed to lean heavily into the Polynesian pop aesthetic, but its downtown location and revenue needs forced it to change into a far more lucrative club-like atmosphere. Shore Leave, also in Boston, started off as a tiki bar, but due to worries about cultural appropriation, the underground bar eventually shifted concepts toward light tropical.

Other tactics to keep tiki alive in New England met with varying degrees of success. Some bars offered "tiki nights" or dedicated an area of their larger concept to tiki drinks; for example, Ogie's Trailer Park in Providence, Rhode Island, was able to fit a tiki bar into its astounding retro kitsch concept. China Palace in Rochester, New Hampshire, which had been in operation since 1969, added a lightly themed tiki bar when they renovated in 2016. Some bars and restaurants had tiki theme nights or months, like Massachusetts bars Gigantic in Easthampton and Less Than Greater Than in Hudson. Even the Lobby Bar in Cambridge's Hotel Marlowe experimented with tiki overlays (overleis?), yet another place trying on a coat of tropical colors for a while before reverting back to its regular self. Still other new places seemed to bring the 1980s tiki aesthetic into the now: Friki Tiki in Branford, Connecticut, and One Eyed Jack's in Worcester, Massachusetts, come to mind—places that are ostensibly tiki but that eschew the vibe of hidden escape and the look of classic tiki destinations like the original Aku-Aku or the Polynesian Village. You'll find some tiki masks and usually a lot of thatch, but the spirit of tiki is lost in the party. It's the ornamentation of tiki without the atmosphere of tiki.

Societies sprang up in this new world of tiki. One "cult within a cult" is the Fraternal Order of the Moai (FOM), a group of like-minded tiki fans in Columbus, Ohio, formed in 2000 from the ashes of the sadly shuttered Kahiki Supper Club, the state's immense temple of tiki. "The mission of the Fraternal Order of Moai," the mission statement reads, "is to serve as the premier fraternal organization and social network for all men and women interested in tiki culture and the Polynesian pop era; to spread the aloha spirit."

Despite the outsized legacy of the Kahiki, its gravity could not keep the FOM tied only to Ohio, and other chapters emerged around the country and in other parts of the world. Two years after the FOM's inception, the Queequeg Chapter—named for the character in *Moby-Dick*, continually a tiki reference point—was chartered in New England. The FOM presents the illusion of operating like a secret society, requiring new members to be sponsored by current members; there's a secret initiation ritual, and members refer to each other by tiki-centric monikers. Honored members (aka the Honui) get to wear fetching blue fezzes emblazoned with the FOM logo and sporting a long tassel. It's stuff like this that makes the new community of tiki so much fun, combining and recontextualizing classic American traditions and updating them to a present sensibility with a sense of humor and a more enlightened view of the past.

Despite these feints toward old-fashioned secret clubs, one of FOM's goals is extremely public facing: supporting their communities through charitable acts and giving. The Fraternal Order of the Moai Foundation started a decade after the club's inception and helps support the communities of which they're a part. Some of that is through fundraising and charity events. Some is through supporting local tiki bars, restaurants, and lounges. Both types usually involve at least a little rum.

Starting in 2007 and going through 2014, the FOM also sponsored the Northeast Tiki Tour, a semi-annual event that brought tikiphiles from all over to the region's best and most important tiki haunts. One of the issues with growing real tiki roots in New England is that it's a deceptively large place. Whereas in a place like San Francisco, you can walk one hundred feet in any direction and hit a tiki bar, in New England, you have to be targeted and specific and be willing to travel great distances in order to go to a second tiki location. Given its size, history, and importance, most of the tours featured Kowloon—New England's tiki Jupiter—as one of its stops, with the rest within its orbit. The Bali Hai, the South Pacific, the Ho Kong, and Tiki Island with its lobby moai were among the stops. And for real history of the South Pacific, New England has the Peabody Essex Museum, ready to offer some bracing real-world history to these invented spaces.

One other fascinating trend comes out of the craft cocktail movement. Now that classic tiki drinks have had their revival as worthy contemporaries to the Sidecar and the Manhattan, some bars have introduced their interpretations of the Mai Tai, the Zombie, and others as part of their elevated menu, without the need for the trappings of tiki. Eastern Standard in Boston served Zombies, Trader Vic's Punch, and a Brother Cleve original, the Cactus Flower. Baldwin Bar, part of Sichuan Garden in Woburn, Massachusetts, offers three types of crafted Mai Tais along with a libations menu to rival that of California's Zombie Village or Forbidden Island. Baldwin Bar is retro in a classy way, leaning into the dark wood and sophisticated accoutrements of an old-style gentlemen's club. It's the opposite of the party ambience of some of the more tiki-lite places that emphasize beer and burgers along with their rum drinks, treating cocktails seriously and deliciously but without all that silly islandy stuff to get in the way.

So New England is at a crossroads. Are we a region content to let the full Polynesian pop experience languish, putting together our own personal environmental mixtapes of our favorite tiki elements and discarding the rest?

One possible solution is chef and owner Jason Doo's Wusong Road. Opened in early 2022 in Cambridge, Massachusetts, it's an elevated version of New England's ubiquitous Chinese American restaurants with tiki drinks. For one, Wusong Road has two actual tiki bars, one tucked into the back of the second floor and one dominating the more immersive space on the ground floor. Both bars feature an extensive rum selection and bartenders who understand how to use them. Lamps ringed in thatch hang from the ceilings, TV screens purport to be windows looking out on tropical vistas, and a glassed-in case packed with tiki mugs from all over the country and throughout tiki's long history stands at the first-floor entryway. Upstairs, a huge poster for the film version of *Kon-Tiki* hangs beside a doorway lined with actual jade tiles, and a massive gong emblazoned with the Wusong Road logo—a dragon winding itself into a circle—dominates the back of the second-floor bar.

Climbing up from street level, you're immediately in a whole new environment: the stairwell is a jungle, and monkeys of various sizes emerge out of the gloom, some even holding the lamps that light your way. All around, light exotica music suffuses the atmosphere with animal sounds calling out. By

Wusong Road gong and back bar. *Gabriel Bascom.*

the time you pass through the restaurant area and approach the bar, the music picks up, remaining tropical but with a little more pep and verve.

When Wusong Road first opened, the second floor was the only place you could really get into the tiki mindset. The first floor was initially set up as a fast-casual Chinese restaurant, but as Doo's confidence in his concept grew, he realized that a full tiki immersion was the way to go. Over the course of a few months, he fully renovated the first floor, making it a true tiki lounge. Now you can find couches, comfortable bar seats, and that ineffable feel of permanent dusk, with indirect lighting and the windows hidden from view—all of which invite patrons to stay a while and get lost in the atmosphere of escape.

Wusong Road also became the hub for the emergent New England Tiki Society, a loose gathering of tiki-minded people who meet once a month for events. In between jaunts to Wusong Road, Kowloon, and more, they trade

Wusong Road outside sign. *Gabriel Bascom.*

cocktail recipes and share rum purchases and home-bar décor tips online. It's the existence of a group like this that makes it feel like tiki is finally here to stay in New England: a society that appreciates and is curious about the deep, sometimes convoluted past of Polynesian pop, revels in the present, and works to preserve the best parts of tiki for the future.

Beyond the bars and cocktails, the mugs and fish float lamps, tiki in America is made up of people looking for a unique way to escape the sometimes-overwhelming world outside. And it's in people, the diverse Yankee melting pot that makes up Maine, Massachusetts, Rhode Island, Connecticut, Vermont, and New Hampshire, that New England tiki lives.

INTERVIEW WITH JASON DOO, OWNER OF WUSONG ROAD

Tell me a little bit about you—how long have you been a chef? Where did you get your start? Did you know a tiki restaurant was going to be in your future?
I started in my family's Chinese American restaurant in Malden, Massachusetts, called Bobo's when I was just a kid. From there, I went to university but decided to pursue a culinary career and went to work for the Intercontinental Hotel in Boston. From there, I went to work for the Fairmont and eventually wound up at Menton before leaving for New York City. In NYC, I worked in a few hotels in Brooklyn and eventually made my way to

Asia. From there, I came back and worked as the director of operations for a farm-to-table restaurant group where I was eventually canned and decided to open my own restaurant. COVID struck, construction prices skyrocketed, staffing sucked, prices for food, liquor, and utilities shot through the roof. Perfect timing really [laughs].

What has your involvement with the world of tiki been before the restaurant? Was the tiki revival of the 1990s (and still ongoing) a big influence on you?
Nothing whatsoever. I didn't know Tiki culture was a thing, honestly. I just really loved growing up in my parents' restaurant, playing on the delivery slide, drinking Shirley Temples from tiki mugs, shooting darts with the locals, and eating crab rangoons. Everyone always seemed like they were having fun and just liked hanging out chatting with each other.

What were your inspirations for Wusong Road, both food/drink wise and theme wise?
Honestly, to just open a good bar—not a craft cocktail spot where everyone wears vests and ties, not a place where chefs plate with tweezers, but a good old-fashioned bar serving some fun American Chinese food. Theming? A place to showcase my small collection of tiki mugs that were getting dusty on my shelves at home and trying to capture the look and feel of some of my favorite restaurants I saw in Asia while backpacking with friends when I was younger.

Wusong Road monkey lamp. *Gabriel Bascom.*

Did you have any concerns over using the word "tiki" for Wusong Road, especially given its location and possible backlash?

Haha, yes, we've received backlash on so many fronts. We have people accusing us of stealing Hawaiian culture (note, we have no Hawaiian Tiki statues; everything we have are from my personal collection from Burma, Indonesia, Thailand, China, Japan, etc.). We also have so many comments on how "inauthentic" we are and even had an article written about how "clean" our restaurant bathrooms were and how that isn't authentic (seriously, what the hell). Even in one scenario, I had a manager of another bar (a former tiki bar who rebranded to a "tropical bar" located here in Boston)—who is white and identifies as LGBTQ—call us out on Instagram stating how we do not support people of color community or LGBTQ community (the person didn't even do enough research to see that I'm actually a person of color and identify as LGBTQ). Every day, I also have to read through negative comments and emails stating how "we are a cheap Chinese restaurant that is shabby and looks like we dug through the trash at the Kowloon," or, "Another overpriced Chinese takeout place serving only frozen food and uses drink mixes." So I either am not authentically Asian enough or we are not authentically Asian American food enough, or we are not tiki enough. The tiki community can also be a bit much for us. We get some people that will not even visit us because we do not play exotica music 24/7 or have tikis everywhere carved by X artists. It can be mentally draining to be torn in so many directions, but I think the restaurant, and myself, have finally started to mature enough where we have decided to walk down our own road, Wusong Road (see what I did there?).

Why do you think it's been so difficult to get a tiki scene going in New England? Adherence to the original tenets of tiki—something I think Wusong does well and is getting even better at—seems to fall by the wayside for many new places, which prefer a party atmosphere to the feel of tropical escape. What led you to go the more traditional route?

I didn't even consider the bar traditional tiki; I would say we are more tiki adjacent with a flair for Asiatica (because that's what I just collected). In the end, I love the textures of bamboo, rattan, woods, and warm lighting. Mix in some brass touches and some tropical flowers, and BAM, you got yourself a bar that looks pretty damn tiki.

Where do you see tiki going in the future, especially in New England?

Niche; most of our customers do not really know, or I think care, what tiki or tiki culture is. They just want to have a tropical drink, relax, and have a good time in a restaurant with a good ambiance. Little do they know they are living the tenets of tiki!

EPILOGUE

The Kahiki Supper Club in Columbus, Ohio, one of the world's foremost tiki temples, closed its doors in August 2000. In 2020, Kansas City's TikiCat, one of the best and most promising new tiki establishments, closed for good. We've already seen what happened to so many New England tiki places like Aku-Aku, Rhum, Kahiki Moon, Kon-Tiki Ports, and all the rest. Exciting tiki and Polynesian pop places have been unable to stand the test of time or the rigors of operating a slice of fantasy in an uncaring real world.

But through it all, our Kowloon has remained standing. It weathered the height of the pandemic by becoming a temporary drive-in and carhop service, showing classic movies on a huge twenty-two-foot-high, forty-foot-wide screen and serving the whole menu, including cocktails. When it reopened its doors, customers surged back inside; it even hosted one of the first New England Tiki Society meet-ups. Kowloon is a mainstay, a fixture in the New England tiki topography.

Except that may be changing.

As reported by the site Boston Restaurant Talk on January 7, 2021:

> *Representatives* [of the restaurant] *met with planning board officials tonight to announce the eventual closing of the restaurant and a redevelopment of the property into* [multiple] *lots for mixed use. Bobby Wong spoke on behalf of Kowloon and stated that there are no dates to close and the closure will not come before a process of getting approvals for the project and initiating the project. Kowloon has no date to close.*

Later, owner Bobby Wong clarified the statement, emphasizing, "We are not sold or closing soon.…We are only planning for the future which will be years not months away.…We have just completed our 70th year in business and realize that though rewarding, it's such a demanding life. And there will be an end at some point…just not right now."

The capricious nature of tiki in New England may yet claim one of our most recognizable landmarks. There may never be another like Kowloon, a tiki destination for generations of New Englanders. Will there ever be another tiki surge all the way out here in the northern Atlantic states? One that necessitates building a place like Kowloon, with thousands of seats, a classic Midcentury A-frame, and a massive carved idol, constantly holding sway over all it surveys? Maybe not. But never say never. Tiki has disappeared and returned even stronger in the past. Who's to say what the future will bring?

Thanks to Brother Cleve (1955–2022)
I hope there are Mai Tais in heaven.

BIBLIOGRAPHY

Admin, Dycella. "'The Best for the Most for the Least': The Eames Office and the Democratic Impulse." Jim Carroll's Blog, November 15, 2020. www.jimcarrollsblog.com/blog/2018/11/22/the-best-for-the-most-for-the-least-the-eames-office-and-the-democratic-impulse.

ArtInRuins. "Chinese Restaurants of the Past." 2008. artinruins.com/property/chinese-restaurants.

Auffrey, Richard. "The Origins of the Pupu Platter." Sampan, December 3, 2021. sampan.org/2021/history/the-origins-of-the-pupu-platter.

Belliveau, Chelsea. "The Story of the Cocoanut Grove Fire." Boston Fire Historical Society, April 16, 2021. bostonfirehistory.org/the-story-of-the-cocoanut-grove-fire.

Berry, Jeff. *Beachbum Berry's Sippin' Safari: In Search of the Great "Lost" Tropical Drink Recipes…and the People behind Them.* N.p.: Cocktail Kingdom, 2017.

Blakemore, Erin. "The Tragic Story of America's Deadliest Nightclub Fire." History.com, A&E Television Networks, November 27, 2017. www.history.com/news/the-tragic-story-of-americas-deadliest-nightclub-fire.

Bock, Jon. "Skipper Kent and the Zombie Village." Williams Gallery West Collectibles, the Skipper Kent Collection History, 1998. galwest.com/collectibles/skipper_kent/history.htm#:~:text=All%20told%2C%20Frank%20%22Skipper%22,the%20Trans%2DPacific%20Yacht%20Race.

Boston Herald. "Throwback Thursday: Raise a Glass to Boston's Stylish Past." December 31, 2015. www.bostonherald.com/2015/12/31/throwback-thursday-raise-a-glass-to-bostons-stylish-past.

Cate, Martin, and Rebecca Cate. *Smuggler's Cove: Exotic Cocktails, Rum and the Cult of Tiki.* N.p.: Ten Speed Press, 2016.

Curtis, Wayne. *And a Bottle of Rum: A History of the New World in Ten Cocktails.* N.p.: Crown Publishers, 2006.

Danna, Nicole. "The Hukilau Returns for Annual Tiki Takeover at Pompano Beach's Beachcomber Resort." *Miami New Times*, May 26, 2022. www.miaminewtimes.com/restaurants/the-hukilau-returns-to-south-florida-for-its-21st-year-of-tiki-cocktails-and-seminars-14516058#:~:text=Billed%20as%20%E2%80%9CThe%20World%27s%20Most,to%20the%20event%20through%202016.

Dinneen, Joseph F. "Spilling the Beans." *Boston Globe*, December 30, 1942, 8.

Dobbs, G. Michael. "Hu Ke Lau to Close April 6, Then Be Reborn." *Reminder Publications*, March 8, 2018. www.thereminder.com/localnews/chicopee/hu-ke-lau-to-close-april-6-then-be-reborn.

First, Devra. "A New Generation of Chefs Is Embracing—and Updating—the Classic American Chinese Restaurant." *Boston Globe*, January 26, 2022.

Fleming, Daniel J. "The Cocoanut Grove Revisited." National Archives and Records Administration, 2017. www.archives.gov/publications/prologue/2017/fall/cocoanut-grove.

Goldfarb, Aaron. "All the Tiki That's Fit to Print." PUNCH, May 26, 2020. punchdrink.com/articles/fit-to-print-tiki-news-magazine.

Henderson, Jason, and Adam Foshko. *California Tiki: A History of Polynesian Idols, Pineapple Cocktails and Coconut Palm Trees.* Charleston, SC: The History Press, 2018.

Henderson, Rabekah. "What Is Witco? The History of the Iconic Tropical Furniture Maker." Home, June 29, 2021. www.atomic-ranch.com/interior-design/witco.

Humuhumu. "Guide to Tiki Bars and Polynesian Restaurants." Critiki, 2017. critiki.com.

Hurwitz, Marc. "Subdivision Plan Reportedly Discussed for Kowloon Space in Saugus." Boston Restaurants, January 7, 2021. bostonrestaurants.blogspot.com/2021/01/subdivision-plan-reportedly-discussed.html?fbclid=IwAR2ATx7-pfk0mOd-NYPJUjUylZV2EgzbV9b8JrKQcADHLXgsdptmMN5NLXE&m=1.

Kirsten, Sven A. *The Book of Tiki: The Cult of Polynesian Pop in Fifties America.* N.p.: Taschen, 2003.

———. *Tiki Modern:…and the Wild World of Witco.* N.p.: Taschen, 2007.

———. *Tiki Pop: America Imagines Its Own Polynesian Paradise = Tiki Pop: L'Amérique rêve Son Paradis Polynésien.* N.p.: Taschen, 2014.

McGerick, Scott. "Scott McGerik's Collections." Orchids of Hawaii. collections.mcgerik.com/collection/orchids-of-hawaii.

New York Times. "Four Men Indicted as Leaders of Huge Liquor Ring." January 5, 1933, 44.

Ostrander, Gilman. "The Colonial Molasses Trade." *Agricultural History* 30 (1956): 77–84.

Pan, Deanna. "The Legacy of Kowloon." *Boston Globe*, October 18, 2022, 1–18.

Peabody Essex. "Oceanic Art Collection: Over 20,000 Oceanic Objects." www.pem.org/explore-art/oceanic-art.

Peaslee, Erica. *Out to Sea: The Cultural Impact of New England's Maritime History*. Huntsville, TX: Sam Houston University, 2014. www.academia.edu/30430580/Out_to_Sea_The_Cultural_Impact_of_New_Englands_Maritime_History.

Recarte, Ana. *Historical Whaling in New England*. University of Alcala, Madrid, Spain. Friends of Thoreau. institutofranklin.net/sites/default/files/2021-03/CS%20Whaling%20in%20New%20England.pdf.

Sable, Jeanne Prevett, et al. "The Great Boston Molasses Flood, Prohibition and Anarchists." Forgotten New England, April 18, 2021. forgottennewengland.com/2020/12/16/the-great-boston-molasses-flood-prohibition-and-anarchists.

Sapka, Steve. "Robert 'Brother Cleve' Toomey, 'Godfather of Boston's Bar Scene' and Global Tastemaker, Dies at Age 67." Associated Press, September 19, 2022. apnews.com/article/boston-massachusetts-obituaries-319238044f16314a421f04dd5fb5c399.

Schell, Scott. "Collector's Corner: The Amazing Adventures of Skipper Kent." *Tiki Magazine and More*, June 2017, 44–51.

Sohn, Emily. "Why the Great Molasses Flood Was So Deadly." History.com, A&E Television Networks, January 15, 2019. www.history.com/news/great-molasses-flood-science.

Star-Bulletin. "'Beachcomber' Name Is Ruled Owned by 'Don.'" May 23, 1941, 1.

Stern, Jane, and Michael Stern. "Orchids of Hawaii." *New Yorker*, July 2, 1989, 27–28.

Stone, David Norton. "Chapter 2—Themed." *Lost Restaurants of Providence*. Charleston, SC: The History Press, 2019.

Sunday Herald. "New Polynesian Restaurant." November 5, 1961.

Thomas, Jack. "The Cocoanut Grove Inferno." *Boston Globe*, November 22, 1992, 1.

Wieczorek, Rafal. "Two Unusual Moko Figurines from the Peabody Essex Museum in Salem." *Rapa Nui Journal* 30, no. 1 (2016): 13–18. doi.org/10.1353/rnj.2016.0002.

ABOUT THE AUTHOR

Kevin Quigley is the author of the novels *Meatball Express*, *I'm on Fire*, and *Roller Disco Saturday Night*, as well as the short story collections *Damage & Dread* and *This Terrestrial Hell*. His stories have appeared in the Cemetery Dance anthologies *Halloween Carnival* and *Shivers*, the bestselling *Shining in the Dark* anthology, the thriller collection *Death of a Bad Neighbour*, and Lawrence Block's upcoming *Playing Games*.

Quigley is also known for his monographic work on Stephen King (including *The Stephen King Illustrated Movie Trivia Book*, *Chart of Darkness*, and *Stephen King Limited*) and for *The Sound Sent Shivers Down My Back*, a deep exploration into the Oregon folk-rock band Blitzen Trapper and their seminal album *Furr*. He lives in Boston, Massachusetts, with his husband, Shawn.